7 STEPS TO TURN YOUR
DARKNESS
INTO LIGHT

God's Plan for Addictions, Jails, and Other Dark Places.

CHAPLAIN
Patrick Day

PYRAMID
Publishers

Minneapolis, Minnesota
patrickday@pyramidpublishers.com

Printed by Lightning Source
1246 Heil Quaker Blvd. La Vergne, TN USA 37086
ISBN – 978-0-9982014-7-4

Cover Design by Myron Sahlberg
Drawings by Myron Sahlberg
Interior Design by Van-garde Imagery, Inc.
Printed in the United States of America

The men and women in this book are all real people with real problems, impacted by Jesus Christ, who died on the cross for their sins 20 centuries ago. I've personally interacted with all of them over extended periods of times. I've changed their names and enough of the details so only they would be able to recognize themselves.

CHAPLAIN
Patrick Day

My Own Prison of Darkness

I know darkness on a personal basis. From the spring of 2006 to the winter of 2010, I endured a deep, all-encompassing depression so horrific that I longed for death. At first, total darkness surrounded me. Then slivers of light began to appear.

For the first two years, depression was my perpetual prison, my addiction, and the darkest place imaginable. Nothing brought any light. I sunk in a reclining chair for hours on end, unable to read anything or watch TV — like a corpse lying in a casket. I couldn't sleep, eat, or bring ease to my body. I left the house as little as possible. It was also very hard on my family.

I'd been a born-again believer for 25 years and thought God and I were buddies. I faithfully read the Bible, went to church religiously, and was in the same Christian men's group for more than 20 years. I made sure both my boys went to Sunday School and church, even when they didn't want to do so.

But there wasn't much depth to my relationship with God the Father and His Son, Jesus Christ. I'd been paddling about in the shallows. When depression struck, I wasn't spiritually equipped for it. I was like a man sinking in quicksand, unable to pull myself out and unsure how to seek help. I wasn't stable enough to engage with God, read the Bible, or pray. The darkness was too powerful.

In desperation, I begged God to help me, but I couldn't get close enough to Him to hear His voice. In the fall of 2007, after a total shoulder replacement, my right arm was paralyzed for a month and the darkness overwhelmed me. At my lowest point, I declared to God, "I give up. I put myself in Your hands."

That's what He wanted to hear, I guess. A peace washed over me at a point in my life where hope was nowhere to be found. A neurologist had told me I'd regain the feeling in my arm, but I didn't believe him. I feared my arm would be paralyzed forever. When I gave up on myself and trusted in God, I knew my arm would be healed, and it was.

God's loving-kindness kicked into gear, and He became involved in my life more than I could've imagined. I wasn't healed in a flash, but my journey to recovery had started. I fired a mean and incompetent psychiatrist who had done me more harm than good. The next day, God led me to a wonderful psychiatrist who found the right combination of medications to start stabilizing me. At the same time, the Lord put an empathetic and wise psychotherapist in my path who helped heal my mind, will, and emotions. A few months later, a godly minister prayed with me and anointed me.

In summary, my healing was a three-legged stool that continued for three years until I made my final escape from depression. Stabilization for my brain chemistry by medication came first. The healing of my heart and soul through psychotherapy followed. And finally I experienced spiritual healing by the Light Who shines in the darkness.

My final escape from the terrible darkness of depression into the light of sanity ultimately came by following the 7 steps presented in this book. I renewed my salvation, aligned myself with God's True North, put Jesus first in my life, started reading the Bible daily again, and prayed like my life depended on it. My God became my all in all.

I've written a book about my darkness and finding the light of life. It's called *How I Escaped from Depression* and is available on Amazon. If I escaped the darkness, so can you!

Table of Contents

Chapter One
What difference does Jesus make?

In the beginning was the Word [Jesus], and the Word was
with God, and the Word was God... In Him was life and
that life was the light of all mankind. The light shines in the
darkness, and the darkness has not overcome it.

John 1:1-5

DARKNESS AND LIGHT

Darkness and light battle over every square inch of physical, mental, and spiritual territory on this planet, and everything in your life hinges on whether you align yourself with the darkness or with the light.

The battlefield is in your soul – that is, your mind, will, and emotions – and overshadows every path on which you step. You can never rest; it's always warfare. If you do nothing, the darkness will swallow you up whole.

If you want to turn your darkness into light, you need to have a plan with defined steps – seven sounds about right.

I have come into the world as a light, so that no one who
believes in me should stay in darkness.

John 8:12

The arrival of Jesus into this world divided history into two separate periods of time:

B.C. Before Christ.

A.D. Anno Domini, which is Latin for "in the year of our Lord"; that is, the year Jesus was born.

Who is this Jesus who divided history in two and what difference does He make in the lives of His creation?

Is His merely a story that happened two thousand years ago, or does He have real significance in this present age? Let's examine two lives that were turned from darkness into light by Jesus Christ.

MARIE'S STORY

Marie was swimming toward a darkness that would end up drowning her, but she didn't realize it at the time.

The day she turned sixteen, her friends threw a birthday bash for her that included alcohol and meth. She stumbled through the front door the next morning at 3 a.m., three hours past her curfew, and her parents grounded her for two weeks. She stayed downstairs in her bedroom all that day. At times she was sad, but mostly she was mad. Sometimes she cuddled up with Pinky, her stuffed elephant, and Briscoe, her stuffed bear. Sometimes she hurled them against the wall in anger.

Her boyfriend called later that afternoon.

"Hey, Muffin, there's one great party going down tonight where we was. You gotta be there."

"I can't go anyplace for two weeks," she answered in a huff.

After a short pause came a tempting voice out of the darkness.

"Hey, girl, whattaya gonna do – let your parents rule ya or take charge of your own life? I'll stop by at 10 tonight and hang out in my car while you make your getaway. Don'tcha disappoints me."

When 10 o'clock arrived, Marie went upstairs and stood by the front door.

"Where are you going?" her father asked in a quiet voice.

"Out!" she yelled, with a glare that froze them in place.

"You're not going to tell *me* what I can and can't do. I'm old enough to make my own decisions. I'm leaving."

"Please don't go," her mother pleaded. "We love you and only want what's best for you."

"No, you don't love me. You hate me. You don't want me to have any fun."

Her face quivered and started to turn red as she stood with her hand on the doorknob.

Marie had a choice to make – light or darkness, good or evil. She could obey her parents and her God and go back downstairs to her bedroom. Or she could go the way of Adam and Eve and do her own thing, in willful disobedience.

"I'm leaving," she proclaimed defiantly, "and I'm never coming back home, ever."

She made good on that promise. At the age of sixteen, Marie started a life of drugs and alcohol and ended up living in a meth house owned by a guy named Kenny. Three *kind of* couples shared the three-bedroom home – Kenny and his girlfriend, Shawn and his girlfriend, and Marie and Pete. Who stayed with whom varied from week to week.

When Marie was eighteen, after nearly dying from an overdose, she caught a glimpse of the darkness surrounding her and turned back to the light. She called her parents and asked if she could come home. Their prayers were answered. They could hardly contain their excitement.

Marie returned home and took a part-time job in an assembly plant near her home. She finished her high school degree at an area learning center and stayed as sober as sober could be. To celebrate her graduation and one-year anniversary of not using, her parents brought her to a fancy restaurant.

Most of her high school class had gone on to college. The ones she hung around with stumbled through high school and stayed local, working in low-paying jobs to earn enough money to exist and buy drugs. One of them worked at that very restaurant. Zack came out from the kitchen and sauntered over to their table. "Hey, Muffin, there's a great party coming down this Friday at my place. Why don't you swing by and catch up with the old gang?"

If looks could kill, Zack would be six-feet under, done in by the glare of Marie's parents. "I can't do that, Zack," said Marie. "I'm sober now, and that's the way I'm going to stay." Her parents smiled as they held hands underneath the table.

Zack shrugged his shoulders. "Whatever, but if you change your mind, I live at 3200 Chowen Lane in Edina. Things are hopping at my place every Friday and Saturday night."

"I won't change my mind, Zack. I've a new life now." Her response was how she honestly felt at the moment, but the seed of temptation had been planted in her mind where it slowly grew into a small thorn bush that agitated her consciousness for the next month.

Now that she had finished her high-school degree, she had time on her hands, and watching wheel of fortune with her parents was getting old. To those who had gone on to college and the few who stayed around and never used, she was *The Meth Girl* who ran away from home. They wanted nothing to do with her.

On a weekend her parents were out of town, Marie sat in the living room as bored as bored could be. "Maybe I should go over to Zack's and see the old gang," she thought. "But I'm not going to take any drugs."

For the next two months, she was a regular at Zack's house every Friday and Saturday night. Her parents cried a lot and sighed a lot as they saw their daughter return to a life of drugs. They pleaded with her to get help, but Marie turned another page in her *I'll do it my way* book. "You're going to hound me to death. I need to get out of here."

One week later, she and Susie drove to Los Angeles for a change of scenery. Neither one could get a job because they couldn't pass background checks. They ran out of their meager supply of money and had a choice to make: sell their bodies or sell meth on the streets. They chose to sell meth.

Susie got busted six weeks later and sent to the LA County Jail. Marie decided to change careers. Transporting small amounts of heroin and moving stolen cars and other goods from LA to inland cities was safer and paid better, until the police arrested her for driving a stolen car and third degree drug possession. For the next 15 years, Marie was in and out of California state prisons and jails for violating parole, drug possession, burglary, writing bad checks, and transporting stolen property. In her own words, she was hard-core bad.

She became as tired as tired could be of prisons and jails. "This time I'm going to stay sober for the rest of my life," she'd promise, but within a month she was using again. Then came, "Maybe I can't stay off drugs, but I can be a functional addict and keep a job and stay away from crime." That didn't work so well either.

In a Northern California prison, her cellmate invited her to a Sunday-afternoon Bible study. She thought, "Why not? What do I have to lose?" Three months later, she accepted Jesus Christ as her Savior and put Him in charge of her life. She called her parents and told them she was saved. They told Jessica – a person from their church who was a drug counselor – about their daughter, and she started writing to Marie in prison. Over the course of 16 months, they formed a strong bond between them.

Jessica had her Bible study group of women pray furiously for Marie, including a prayer warrior named Annie. When Marie executed her sentence, she moved back to Minnesota and moved in with Jessica in Minnetonka.

Marie was now a born-again Christian and her life of crime went away, but she still craved meth in the worst way. Jessica suggested Marie check out a faith-based rehabilitation center in South Minneapolis called Adult and Teen Challenge. But after 15 years of incarceration, Marie didn't want to put her life on hold for another year. Jessica kept promoting; Marie kept resisting.

Jessica told stories of addicts she counseled who were changed dramatically by Adult and Teen Challenge, and she suggested that Marie needed to become addicted to Jesus instead of meth — all with a smile instead of a frown. Marie understood that Jessica loved her and wanted what was best for her. "You win," said Marie. "I'll drive over there today. Are you happy now?"

After an hour of driving around South Minneapolis trying to find the facility, Marie's car sputtered with the sound a car makes when it's on its last quart of gas. Marie saw a gas station on the next block and pulled up to a pump just as her motor quit. She had no money but had plenty of anger and frustration. It crossed her mind to fill up the car and drive off, but the station was in a bad neighborhood and was pre-pay only.

A woman on the other side of the pump asked if she could help her. Marie started crying uncontrollably. "I promised Jessica I'd visit a place called Adult and Teen Challenge around here someplace. She said that would be my best bet to overcome my drug addiction, but now I'm lost and out of gas and out of patience and..." She couldn't go on.

The woman stopped filling her car and proceeded to put half of her pre-paid gas into Marie's tank. "I work at the Adult and Teen Challenge you're looking for," the woman said. It's only two blocks from here. By the way, does the Jessica you referred to live in Minnetonka?"

Marie nodded her head. "How did you know?"

"Because I'm one of the women who's been praying for you the past year. You must be Marie." Marie's jaw about dropped to the base of the gas pump. "I'm Annie. Have you heard of me?" Marie remembered Jessica talking about an Annie who prayed up a storm for her and nodded her head. "Drop by tomorrow at 10 a.m. and I'll personally give you a tour and answer all her questions."

Marie agreed to come the next day – but not just to tour the facility. She knew she'd been touched by God, and her reluctance to put her life on hold for 13 months flew out the window. She signed into Adult and Teen Challenge the next day. It was exactly what she needed. Gradually her hunger for drugs disappeared and was replaced by a hunger for Jesus Christ and all He had to offer. When she completed the program, they hired her as an outreach staff member who went to jails and prisons to inform inmates and prisoners that Adult and Teen Challenge could be their best bet to get off drugs and put their lives back together.

The last I heard about Marie, she was changing the lives of inmates and addicts throughout Minnesota by giving her testimony and offering them hope. Did Christ make a difference in Marie's life? You betcha. And He can turn around your life as well, if you trust Him with all your heart and lean not on your own understanding.

Chapter Two
Why am I such a sinner?

The world cannot hate you, but it hates me because I testify that its works are evil.

John 7:7

EVIL AND GOOD

If the works of the world are evil, is that not where the darkness originates? And if the Kingdom of God is good, where else would the light proceed from?

The Bible should have a story behind the presence of both evil and good on Earth, but where would you find it? The word *Genesis* in Hebrew means *in the beginning of.* That would probably be a good place to look.

MATT'S STORY PART 1

Ten government-issue stacking chairs formed a semi-circle in a programs room at the Wright County Jail in Buffalo, Minnesota. Inmates who'd signed up for a Sunday-afternoon Gideons Bible study occupied nine of the chairs. The empty tenth chair sat farthest from the door.

"Any questions before we begin?" I asked the group of nine.

A hand went up.

"Can you explain what a born-again believer is? It came up in church this morning."

With the first words *Can you*, a scruffy man shuffled in who looked like he'd just come from his mother's funeral.

He walked by me, one slow step after another. With his head down, he spoke to the floor in a quiet voice.

"My name's Matt, and I need being born-again, but I gotta forgive myself first."

I spoke in a voice that stopped him in his tracks.

"Look at me, Matt! You can't forgive yourself."

I paused for effect, as he stopped dead in his tracks.

"But I've got some really good news for you, Matt. Jesus can forgive you, and He will if you ask Him."

He looked at me with his head cocked to one side, as if I'd just told him the sun would shine at midnight. Then he plodded to his chair, sat down, and remained silent for the next hour.

When the Bible study ended, I pulled Matt aside.

"I'd like to talk to you about being born-again. Would you be willing to meet with me tomorrow, just the two of us?"

"Yep, I guess so. When you find out what I done, maybe not."

He followed the last man out the door, and I stood in the room alone, wondering if he might be my first serial killer.

The next afternoon we met in the jail library, a small room stuffed from floor to ceiling with books and videos. The muscles in his face tightened as he started the conversation.

"You wanna know what I did before you speak your mind?"

"Sure, but you don't need to tell me anything you don't want to. Jesus forgives even the worst of sins."

"Maybe; maybe not."

I felt like a priest in a confessional about to hear that the poor soul on the other side had killed his entire family in a drunken rage.

Matt was stone-faced as he told me he'd been charged with criminal sexual conduct in the 1st degree, with a child under 13.

"You wanna know what's really bad, Chaplain?"

I didn't move or say anything.

"It was my eight-year-old daughter. You wanna know something else really bad?"

What could I say?

"I been watching child porn on my computer and phone, even at work. Couple hours a day anyway, maybe more. That's what made me do it. What I can't figure out, Chaplain, is why I done it. I mean, like, why am I such a sinner?"

Being a chaplain, I'd encountered more than a few cases like this, but never with a person's own child. Yet, it didn't shock me. How could it? In this evil, dark world, anything is possible.

"Sin is sin, Matt, and yours is no worse than King David committing adultery with Bathsheba and then having her husband killed in battle. God forgave his sins, and he'll forgive yours as well."

I may as well have been speaking to the stack of books on the shelves behind Matt. He had his arms folded across his chest and said with a frown on his brow.

"That's not what my pastor says."

"Oh, what does your pastor say?"

"Pastor says 'God hates sin' and 'God's a consuming fire that burns up unpure stuff.' Who's more unpure than me, doing sex stuff with my own daughter?"

Matt looked like a person who'd just purchased a non-cancelable ticket to Hell. His world was dark; there was no light.

"What did your pastor say after that, Matt? Did he talk to you about God forgiving sins no matter how bad they are?"

"Didn't listen after that, Chaplain. I was doin the bad stuff then and knew God hated my sin. Maybe He can unhate some sins, but not ones as bad as mine."

The table between us was as barren as Matt's soul, except for the Bible before me that he kept looking at, as if maybe it had something in it that could help him.

"You don't have to call me Chaplain, Matt. Call me Pat. Do you want to hear the truth, straight from the Bible?"

That wasn't a question that demanded an answer. I knew the following verse by heart, but I opened my Bible to John 3:16 to emphasize that all truth can be found in the pages of the book from which I was reading:

> For God so loved the world that He gave His one and only Son, that whoever believes in Him shall not perish but have eternal life.

"Have you heard that verse before, Matt?"

"Yep. I guess."

"Have you ever asked Jesus to come into your heart?"

He scratched his beard, if you want to call a week of growth a beard, and gave me a blank look.

"What I'm asking you, Matt, is whether you're a real Christian believer or not."

He took his hand away from his face and pointed to the open Bible.

"Yep, I believe in God and Jesus. Been going to church on Sundays with my wife, and my kids're all in Sunday school. Been going to a Bible study Wednesday nights. Guess you'd say I was a Christian. Now I don't think so, I mean with my sin and all. Can't be a Christian and do such terrible things, can I?"

I don't like using the word Christian by itself because of what Matt just said. Being a Christian isn't about keeping rules and regulations, praying before meals, going to church, or anything else we do.

It's about a personal relationship with Jesus Christ. I prefer the words *Christ follower* or *believer* or *born-again Christian* or *real Christian believer*, which is what I used with Matt.

"Going to church and listening to sermons and all the rest of it doesn't make you a Christian, Matt."

His eyes narrowed to slits, and he looked at me like I was from another planet.

"Doesn't make sense, Chaplain, I mean Pat."

"I know it doesn't, Matt, but give me a chance to explain."

"I guess," he answered, without a lick of enthusiasm.

"A little bit ago, you asked me why you were such a sinner. You may as well have asked why I'm such a sinner. You even could have asked why all people enter this world as sinners to start with and shovel sin into their souls like dirt into a ditch."

I now had Matt's full attention. Here was a man uninformed of the story of creation and the sinful nature of all mankind in this fallen world. My job was to inform him of that and nothing more. The rest was up to God.

"What dya mean everyone's a sinner? Where'd that come from? Ain't everyone like me. No way. You aren't."

"I'm as much a sinner as you are, Matt. As to where that comes from, it's all in the Bible, where all truth comes from."

I'm not usually one to quote a bunch of Bible verses to make a point, but I made an exception in this case. Matt needed to hear what God had to say about sin, not what I had to say. In rapid succession I opened my Bible to the following verses.

> *We all, like sheep, have gone astray, each of us has turned to our own way; and the Lord has laid on him the iniquity of us all.*
>
> Isaiah 53:6

Surely I was sinful at birth, sinful from the time my mother conceived me.

Psalm 51:5

For all have sinned and fall short of the glory of God.

Romans 3:23

As for you, you were dead in your transgressions and sins, in which you used to live when you followed the ways of this world and of the ruler of the kingdom of the air, the spirit who is now at work in those who are disobedient.

Ephesians 2:1-2

"Do you believe that the Bible is true, Matt?"

"Yep. I guess so. Would you read them verses again?"

I read them again, slowly, and Matt sat there as if in a trance. The power of God's word had penetrated his mind, and the Holy Spirit had him in His grasp.

"I'm confused about the sinful at birth thing you read."

"Do you want to get unconfused?"

"I guess."

"The answer to the sinful at birth thing can be found in the first three chapters of Genesis."

I walked over to where a row of Bibles were sitting on a shelf and pulled off a New International Version for him, so it would match up with my Bible. I handed it to him, opened up to the first chapter of Genesis.

"Let's look at the very first chapter in the Bible, Matt."

"You mean where God created everything."

"That's it. I want you to look at verses 10, 12, 18, 21, 25, and

31. What do you find in those verses that are almost word for word the same?"

·It didn't take long for Matt to reach a conclusion.

"God saw that it was good."

"That's right, Matt. God saw that His whole creation was good. And that's how he wanted it to remain – good. The second chapter in the Bible tells of the cornerstone of God's creation – mankind. He gave Adam and Eve everything they could possibly want, but he warned them of one thing they couldn't have."

> *You are free to eat of any tree in the garden; but you must not eat from the tree of the knowledge of good and evil, for when you eat of it you will surely die.*

"God loved Adam and Eve with a love that knew no bounds." I paused for effect. "And they loved Him in return. But love isn't love unless there's a choice not to love. That's called free will. Are we okay so far?"

Matt looked at Genesis 2:16-17, shown above, for several seconds before he asked a very smart question.

"If God created everything good, where did evil come from?"

"What do you know about Satan, Matt?"

"He wanted to be like God so God threw him outta Heaven."

"And where did God cast him to?"

If Matt's face were a three-way lightbulb, someone just turned it to the first setting.

"He sent him to Earth. That's where the bad stuff came from. Makes sense now."

"You are right on the mark, Matt. That's where the evil came from in this world. In fact, in John 16:11, Jesus calls Satan *the prince of this world*."

"How can that be, Pat? God created the world. Wouldn't He be the prince of the world or the king or something like that?"

"He would be, but the world turned away from Him?"

"Huh?'

"Let's look at Chapter 3 in Genesis. In the first verse, Satan tempts Eve with the fruit of the tree of the knowledge of good and evil. In the second verse she tells Satan that's the one tree God told them they couldn't eat of. In the third verse, Satan informs her she'd be like God if she ate of its fruit, the very sin he had committed as Lucifer, the most glorious angel in Heaven."

Matt continued to listen intensely, as if he were hearing the 3rd chapter of Genesis the first time.

"Now look at the 6th verse and let's see if Adam and Eve will obey God or listen to Satan's temptation:"

When the woman saw that the fruit of the tree was good for food and pleasing to the eye, and also desirable for gaining wisdom, she took some and ate it. She also gave some to her husband, who was with her, and he ate it.

"That's where your sinful nature comes from, Matt, and where evil and darkness entered the world."

His lightbulb face clicked to the next higher setting.

"So that's the original sin Pastor talked about?"

"You've got it, Matt. Adam and Eve were the first humans and when they disobeyed God, they brought sin into the world and Satan became the prince of the fallen world here on earth.

"So, what do you think God did as a result of their sin? Did He look the other way? Did He forgive them on the spot? What would you have done, Matt?"

"Throwed them outta the garden, like God threw Satan outta Heaven." A slight smile crossed his face for the first time.

"And He did. But there's more to it. Why don't you read Genesis 3:17, Matt?"

To Adam he said, Because you listened to your wife and ate fruit from the tree about which I commanded you, "You must not eat from it," Cursed is the ground because of you.

I could see that the three-way light bulb of Matt's face just switched to the third setting.

"When sin entered the world through Adam and Eve, God cursed the Earth and all that was in it, including Adam and Eve and all their offspring, as in everyone who's ever lived. And He cursed the plants and the animals and the very world itself. That's why we have earthquakes, hurricanes, wildfires, cancer, and evil people who do terrible things. Does all that make sense?"

Matt's mouth was open, and his eyes were bright with understanding.

"Yep. Got it! God meant the world to be good forever and Adam and Eve blew the goodness all to hell. Sorry for swearing, Chaplain. I couldn't help myself."

I laughed.

"It actually wasn't a swear word, Matt. With their sin, Adam and Eve threw away a bright world of goodness and health and made it into a dark world where everyone *is* heading to Hell. That's the fallen world we're born into naturally.

"God is a Holy God who can't look the other way at sin. God hates sin and won't allow anything sinful into His presence. He's also a consuming fire that burns away all impurities either in this world or on the very last day. That's what your pastor meant, not that you can't be forgiven."

I had a large notebook with me and drew the following diagram on a blank page and showed it to Matt:

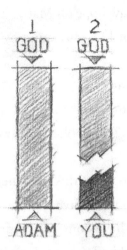

"The first bar represents the normal world as God meant it to be – men and women connected to God. When Adam and Eve sinned, they became separated from God, and the second bar represents the fallen world brought about by their disobedience and pride. And so today, the whole human race is abnormal and wandering this Earth as lost souls in a dark world."

Matt sat at the edge of his chair, and the light bulb of his face changed from 150 watts to 300. What he'd heard in church a hundred times finally made sense to him.

"Pastor talked bout us being like lost sheep; and he quoted some verses in the Bible, but where I don't know."

I remembered where and opened my Bible to Luke 15.

"In this chapter, Jesus talks about lost sheep, a lost coin, and a lost son."

Then I turned to Luke 19 and read verse 10:

For the Son of Man came to seek and to save the lost.

"There you have it. I'm lost, you're lost, we're all of us lost, but Jesus came to find us and save us."

For the first time, I saw hope on Matt's face, and he spoke excitedly.

"Got it. I'm lost, but I can be found by Jesus. Makes sense. Now I'm ready."

"Ready for what, Matt?"

"Ready to be saved or born-again or whatever you call it."

Just then, a program jailer poked his head in the door to make an announcement.

"Sorry, you've got to wrap this up. There's a storm coming, and we'll be going into lockdown in five minutes."

The storm couldn't have come at a worse time. We were on the threshold of salvation and had to stop. I could see Matt was even more frustrated than I was. I collected my thoughts.

"Matt, I normally wouldn't be back for a week, but I'll return tomorrow, so we can talk about being born-again. Until we meet tomorrow, think of what we talked about today. We'll start out tomorrow exactly where we just left off here."

I was worried Satan would work on him through the night and convince him this salvation stuff was a bunch of hooey. I'd seen it happen before. I didn't sleep well that night.

Chapter Three
Step 1: Make sure you're saved.

*When the disciples heard this, they were greatly astonished
and asked, "Who then can be saved?"*

Matthew 19:25

How does anyone become saved? Is it by doing more good than bad or belonging to a church? Do you have to repeat just the right words or go forward for an altar call? Can you be saved by growing up in a Christian home? What does the Bible have to say?

*For it is by grace you have been saved, through faith — and
this is not from yourselves, it is the gift of God — not by
works, so that no one can boast.*

Ephesians 2:8-9

*He saved us, not because of righteous things we had done,
but because of his mercy. He saved us through the washing of
rebirth and renewal by the Holy Spirit.*

Titus 3:5

We don't deserve saving, and there's zero we can do to save ourselves. Salvation comes from God's mercy and grace given to those who...

- Admit they're sinners and kneel in repentance.

- Believe Jesus Christ died on the cross for their sins.

- Ask for forgiveness and accept Jesus as their Savior.

We need only show up with a humble heart and a willingness to be born again. So that's an explanation and a definition, but how does salvation really play out in the actual world?

MATT'S STORY PART 2

My ten-minute trip from my home to the Wright County Jail seemed to take an hour. Hope and courage traveled with me in the front seat, but doubt and fear sat in the back seat taunting me.

Visiting time started at 10 in the morning. On my way down the endless corridor to the Programs area, I prayed the Holy Spirit had set up shop in the library, waiting to save another lost soul. If Matt's salvation depended on me, he'd be a cooked goose.

Matt bounced through the door of the library, and I relaxed. He had an air about him that spoke of great expectations.

"Well, you're looking chipper this morning, Matt. How did you sleep last night?"

"Kinda tossed and turned for bout an hour. Then felt like a warm breeze come into me to calm me down. Like Jesus was sayin, 'It's okay, son, I'm your hope.' It wasn't like real words, you know, more like an echo from somewhere. I mean, like, it probably sounds crazy to you."

Now I felt confident, but not in myself. I could see the Holy Spirit had taken over with Matt. Jesus using the word *hope* with Matt fascinated me. Everyone needs hope, especially men and women who are addicted, in jail, or live in other dark places. In my experience, I've found that Hope is a Somebody, and that Somebody is Jesus Christ.

"No, Matt, it doesn't sound crazy at all. It's the way God works – not with flashing lights and a drum roll but with a whisper that reaches deep into your soul."

Matt's fingers drummed on the table top with anticipation and a bit of impatience.

"Can we get on with it, Pat? Can you save me now?"

The air stalled in my lungs as I settled in my chair. I needed to make an immediate correction to his thinking.

"Matt, you've got something terribly wrong. I can't save you. Only God can save you."

He looked at me with a question mark on his face.

"Huh?"

"Matt, I'm not going to answer your question with my thoughts. Let's see what Scripture says."

I grabbed the Bible in front of me and read Ephesians 2:8-9 (found at the beginning of this chapter).

"Does that make sense to you, Matt?"

"Yep. Kinda. Do you have another verse that might help?"

"I do. Let's take a look at Titus 3:5" (found at the beginning of the chapter after the Ephesians verses).

"I guess maybe I got it now, Pat. I think it's sayin I can't save myself and you can't either."

"That's right, Matt. Only God's grace and mercy can save anyone. Why don't I show you how that works with a drawing."

I opened my notebook to the diagram I'd drawn the day before, added one more piece, and turned it around to show Matt:

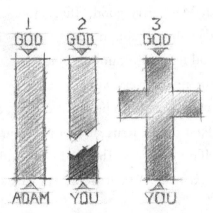

He studied the diagram as if trying to memorize it.

"Okay, Pat, Can you explain what you drawed? I member the first two parts from yesterday, so you don't have to tell me bout them again."

"You remember we talked yesterday about how we can't connect to God in our sinful state. And we can't stand before Him unless we too are holy."

"And there ain't nothin we can do to make that gonna happen, Pat, right?"

"That's right, Matt. You're right on the mark."

Matt couldn't have come up with that on his own. What a blessing for me to see the Holy Spirit in action in the soul of a sinner!

"It looks like the cross is the way to get right with God. But you gotta explain it to me."

"That I will. Though *we* can't bridge the gap by anything we do, God did it for us because He loved us so much. Do you remember John 3:16 from yesterday?"

"For sure; memorized it."

For God so loved the world that He gave His one and only Son, that whoever believes in Him shall not perish but have eternal life.

"That's good, Matt, very good. That's a key verse to memorize. We talked yesterday about being dead in our sins and not being able to stand before God in a sinful, unholy state."

Matt was hanging on every word.

"Those two matters need to be taken care of, and Jesus' death on the cross did it. First of all, Jesus stood in for our sins by taking the curse upon himself on the cross. That's why He said, *My God, My God, why have You forsaken Me*? When we accept His sacrifice for us, our sins are forgiven."

Matt had a confused look on his face.

"What do you mean accepting His sacrifice? If He died for our sins, ain't that enough?"

"Good question, Matt. Let me ask you this. If someone had a gift of a million dollars for you in his hands, what would you do?"

"I'd take it."

"But what if you didn't take it?"

"Then I wouldn't have a million bucks," he said, followed by a thoughtful pause. "Got it. Jesus' death on the cross doesn't do me any good unless I take it. That's the gift of a million bucks."

I smiled. The Holy Spirit was filling his soul with wisdom.

"Worth more than a million dollars, Matt. Much more."

"So the million bucks is forgiveness of my sins? What a deal! Who wouldn't take that?"

"You'd be surprised how many people don't take that. They want to do things their own way, like Adam and Eve."

Matt shook his head in disbelief.

"OK, Pat, got it, I guess. So my sins are forgiven, but you said I can't stand before God unless I'm holy. How does that work? Where in the Bible it says that?"

Conversion comes easy when the Holy Spirit is connecting the dots. And the idea that you need to find answers to questions in the Bible – we all need to understand that.

I'd brought my Amplified New Testament with me for a time like this. From it I read 1 Corinthians 1:30.

But it is from Him that you are in Christ Jesus, who became to us wisdom from God [revealing His plan of salvation], and righteousness [making us acceptable to God], and sanctification [making us holy and setting us apart for God], and redemption [providing our ransom from the penalty for sin].

"You see, Matt, God is holy, but we aren't. Jesus is also holy; and when we choose Him as our representative here on earth instead of Adam, His holiness is credited to us, like a million dollars put into your bank account.

"When we ask Jesus to come into our lives, we stand before God with our sins blotted out and in the holiness of Jesus Christ. We were once a grimy piece of paper that God held in contempt, and He turned His face away. But Jesus erases all the smudges and stains and dirt when we ask Him to be our Savior, and that grimy paper becomes all white and shiny and ready to be written on by the God we've given our life to."

"Like that paper part, Pat. It helps me understand."

I had to laugh to myself. I'd never thought about a dirty and clean sheet of paper before, but the Holy Spirit gave me the image because He knew Matt would grasp a divine mystery with a simple illustration.

I sat up in my chair with my elbows resting on the table. I looked into Matt's eyes as if I were looking into his soul.

"It seems you now understand Christ's death on the cross takes away your sins that have separated you from God and His holiness becomes your holiness. Am I right?"

He didn't hesitate.

"Yep. But I don't feel saved yet?"

"That's because you're not. You now know what the gift is that Christ has in His hand, which we pretended was a million dollars..."

Matt abruptly interrupted me.

"But I ain't taken it yet, right?"

"Right."

"How do I do that?"

"It's as simple as ABC."

With that, I turned to a blank page in my notebook and wrote the letters A and B and C, one letter below another in a vertical column. I turned it around to show Matt.

"The A is for admit. Do you admit the second bar in the drawing represents the condition you're in – born into a sinful nature, which has caused you to sin with abandon? You probably don't have too much trouble with the A."

I was surprised when he put his left hand on the Bible in front of him and raised his right hand.

"I admit I was born with a sinful nature and have sinned right and left since the day I was born. I admit my worst sin was against my own daughter."

Tears came to his eyes. His declaration moved my spirit, but I didn't want to get stuck there, so I went quickly to the B, which stands for believe.

"Do you believe that Jesus is who He says He is – the Way and the Truth and the Life and that no one comes to the Father except through Him? Do you believe He died on the cross for your sins and was resurrected to give you eternal life with Him for all eternity? Do you believe you can stand before God in the holiness of Jesus Christ, your Savior and your Lord?"

His left hand was still on the Bible and his right hand rose as he simply said, "I do," like he was going through a marriage ceremony, which in a way he was.

"Now for the most important part of being born-again." I said, "the C. What do you think that represents?"

Matt had a vacant look on his face, as if I'd asked him for the answer to an ancient riddle. He spoke slowly.

"If the letter was a T instead of a C, I'd say it stood for *Take*, you know as in take the gift. But a C? I can't even guess."

"You're right on target with what you just said, but the C stands for *Choose* instead of *Take*. They both mean the same thing. Maybe I should say *as simple as ABT* in the future?"

Matt laughed.

"Maybe you should. Maybe you should."

It was time to get deadly serious, as in executing the death of the old self and acquiring the birth of the new.

"Do you choose with all your heart and all your soul and all your mind and all your strength to accept Jesus Christ as your Savior and Lord and serve Him only for the rest of your life? Do you choose to be born-again from the natural world of Adam into the spiritual kingdom of Jesus Christ and His Father, through the power of the Holy Spirit?"

Matt's jaw tightened and his right hand shook.

"I choose Jesus Christ as my Savior and accept Him as my Lord. I wanna say goodbye to my old sinful nature from Adam and wanna be born-again into the holiness of Jesus Christ and His Father. I want His gift to me more than anything else I've ever wanted in my life. I wanna be His right now."

At the point of his final declaration, no lights flashed or trumpets blared. And Matt didn't jump out of his chair and holler "Halleluiah!" But the Holy Spirit swept through him like a gentle wind, and Matt knew he was a new creation.

I'd just witnessed another person born-again from a child of sin into a child of God, from Adam's world into the Kingdom of God, from darkness to light. Perhaps the best way of putting it is that he went from being a *me* in the world into being a *we* in the Kingdom of God.

Matt was sentenced to eight years in prison for his crime, and as of the writing of this book, he's more than half way through. He calls me a couple times a month, and I visit him at the prison once a year. He's one of the most solid Christians I know, and I'm thrilled that he's safely tucked away with Jesus both here on Earth and in Heaven to come.

Are you connected to God? Have you accepted Jesus into your heart as Matt did? That's the first step in the seven steps to turn your darkness into light – and the most important one.

If you're not sure you've been reborn of the Spirit, read the last two chapters again and make the best choice possible in this life...to leave the family of man and join the family of God. In doing so, you'll turn your darkness into light.

Chapter Four
Step 2: Plan to go God's way.

Crossroads: a point at which a vital decision must be made.

Some decisions end up being very good for you; others result in something very bad happening. In circumstances both major and minor, you choose darkness or light, evil or good, your way or God's way. It seems one bad choice can lead to another and another and another in a vicious and never-ending cycle.

Let's say a guy named Austin passes a bar he's frequented many times. He'll either go in or not. If he enters, he'll have a drink or look around and leave. If he has a drink, he'll either stop at one or have another. And so it goes until he wakes up in his car the next morning in the parking lot of a golf course, with the motor running and a sheriff's deputy tapping on the window.

From a spiritual standpoint, Austin is either a born-again Christian or he's not. If he's a Christian, he either goes his way or God's way wherever he places his mind or his foot. He endlessly chooses between the world or the Kingdom of God.

How about you? Do you align more with the Kingdom of God or more with the world – in matters both major and minor? The answer, of course, is that it depends. But depends on what?

JASMINE'S STORY PART 1

One afternoon in late November, I met with Jasmine in the programs area of the Wright County Jail. She dragged her body through the classroom door with her eyes on the floor.

She awkwardly sat down in silence, and I asked her, "Jasmine, why do you want to meet with a chaplain?"

Her face came up and her cheeks were wet with tears. Her lips quivered.

"My life is all screwed up. I ask Jesus to help but He don't seem to have time. I'm a mess, a real *mess*."

When she told me her story, *I* started tearing up. Molested as a child, raped more than once as she got older, and battered by two different men with whom she had children. It's little wonder she became a meth and opioids addict.

She described the day she accepted Jesus at a Christian drug rehabilitation center, and it rang true. She had a new self and a new life. But then her old self clawed its way back and started calling the shots.

Think of it this way – you've driven an old run-down car for 20 years and then someone gifts you a brand new car that will never grow old, with Jesus as the chauffeur. You ride in that new car with pride, but then you itch to drive the old car you're so familiar with. You start driving it again, here and there at first, and then most of the time. Eventually, you almost forget you own the new car. That's what happened to Jasmine.

She rode in her new car of redemption, with Jesus at the steering wheel, for a solid year, and the pain in her life became bearable. By and by, loneliness came knocking on her door. She stood by herself all day packaging candy on an assembly line and had no one to go home to at the end of the day except her three children, who needed more attention than she had to give.

One night her loneliness bottomed her out, and she called the father of two of her children to come over and visit. He showed up that very night and didn't leave the next morning, or any other morning for that matter. He brought along with him something she hadn't experienced for about two years – a goodly supply of meth. He also brought along his disposition to yell at the children and slap her around the apartment.

One day it was all too much for her, and she tried some of his meth. By the next day, she was an addict again. He laughed at her because she wasn't, as he said, "holier than thou" any longer. She'd sunk to his level. After a couple of weeks, she was so wasted all the time that he left for greener pastures.

Jasmine begged Willie to leave a few days' worth of meth.

"Sure, baby mom," he said, "but don't you go calling me again. We're through."

Jasmine used up four days of meth in two days. The company she worked for fired her because her addiction represented a danger to herself and others on the assembly line. Mercifully, or not as it ended up, they gave her two weeks' pay.

She spent the money to buy meth and just enough groceries to keep her children and herself alive. One day a social worker showed up and took away her children. Jasmine stood in the doorway as they were led off, too high to even say good-bye.

During the next month, Jasmine smoked enough meth for two people; and she tumbled into a drug-induced psychosis in which she thought everyone wanted to kill her. One day she was driving down a busy road, weaving in and out of traffic like a race driver. A policeman pulled her over, and she thought he wanted to murder her. She jumped into his squad car to escape, was soon caught, and found herself in the jail where we met.

For the first month in jail, she thought the guards wanted to kill her. One morning, reality showed up, and she realized what a pickle she was in. We met two days later, and after telling me her life story, she asked a pointed question.

"Chaplain, why don't Jesus help me? He's a given up on me? What'll I do when I get outta here? I want my children back." She rambled on before giving me a chance to speak.

"Jesus wants to help you, Jasmine, but you're standing in the wrong neighborhood most of the time."

She rubbed her eyes with her fingertips and gave me a curious look.

"Watcha talking about? I'm saved."

"I know that. I'm talking about the two neighborhoods a believer can stand in at any point. In The Kingdom of God, Jesus is king and you follow Him wherever He goes. In the world, you call the shots and ask Jesus to follow you.

"Three years ago you were born-again from the sinful, fallen world into the Kingdom of God, a place where you made good choices. But then you drifted back to the world where you made bad choices."

Jasmine shrugged her shoulders.

"You lost me."

I rose from my chair and walked to the whiteboard.

"Let me draw out what I'm trying to say."

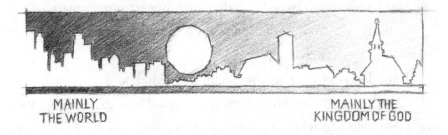

MAINLY
THE WORLD

MAINLY THE
KINGDOM OF GOD

"You're connected to God in either neighborhood, but it's a matter of degree. On the West side of the sun, it's mainly you and the world with some of God thrown in. On the East side of the sun, it's mainly God with some of you and the world thrown in. One side is dark and unstable. The other is light and dependable. Hour by hour and day by day, you choose which neighborhood to stand in. The bad choices you made in the wrong neighborhood put you here in jail."

Jasmine's eyes showed a hint of understanding.

"Cool," she said, "but how about folks who ain't Christians?"

I drew an apple and filled it in with a black marker.

ADAM AND EVE'S DARK WORLD   APART FROM GOD'S LIGHT

"Those people not connected to God by being born-again are like Adam and Eve – separated from God and living in a fallen world. They let events, circumstances, other people, and their own sinful natures control them. When things go bad, they have nowhere to turn except their own thoughts, temptations, and the advice of others. Does that make sense, Jasmine?"

Her hands were clasped together with fingers intertwined.

"I think so, Pat. So you saying I'ma standing in the world when I'm making all those bad choices?"

I nodded yes to her, as I stood by the whiteboard.

"That's exactly what I'm saying. You've asked God to come into your world and help you with all your messes, but that's not how He works. He wants you to come into His kingdom and He'll help you there."

I moved from the board to my chair and leaned back as I said, "Does it make sense now what I'm saying about standing in the wrong neighborhood?'

She nodded her head up and down, with the palms of her hands flat on the table.

"Sure thing. But I got another question. How do I stand in the Kingdom of God and then stay there?" She fidgeted a bit. "I'm sorry for asking stupid questions."

I went from slouching back in my chair to sitting straight up, with my hands on the table to imitate her posture.

"Don't be sorry. It's not a stupid question. Ask me anything."

I don't think Jasmine had been in a situation for a long time where anyone cared what she had to say. I'd just given her permission to be herself, and it was a new experience for her.

"OK, Pat. I know my way don't work. I'm a listenin."

She'd hit the nail right on the head in acknowledging her way didn't work. It's the place all addicts and criminals eventually need to come to for them to have a chance to live a sober life and stay out of jail.

"And your first question, if I understood correctly, is how to stand in the Kingdom of God and how to stay there?"

She drew in a deep breath.

"I guess that's it. Yah, that's it."

"That's the best question you could possibly have asked, Jasmine. It's the perfect question."

Jasmine felt flattered at what I'd just said and broke out into a wide smile. I stood up and went back to the whiteboard.

"When you first got saved, you claimed Jesus was your best friend and you wanted to be with Him everywhere He went. You had a plan, and you depended on that plan to align more with the Kingdom of God than the world. You read the Bible daily and prayed He'd show you what to do with your life. When you got out of rehab, you joined a Spirit-filled church and became part of a Bible study. That's what's called a spiritual plan, and it worked well for you."

I looked at Jasmine and could almost hear the gears turning in her head.

"Suppose I was in the Kingdom of God then."

I hadn't expected her to see the point so quickly.

"And you'd win your bet," I said. "You're one smart cookie."

Jasmine blushed, as if that were the first time in her life anyone had said she was smart. She added, "Somethin else just came at me about back then. I'd surrender myself to Jesus when I got up in the morning and promised to serve others in His name that day."

"Wow!" I exclaimed. You've just painted a perfect picture of what it means to live in the Kingdom of God."

Jasmine smiled at the compliment.

"So what happened that you went back to the world?" I asked, though I knew the answer. She'd misplaced her plan.

"I could do that stuff easy in the rehab place for three months cuz I had time, and I kept trucking through for most a year after that. Then life got in the way. My kids needed taking care of. I had a job. I already told you my boyfriend was gettin high on drugs, and it was easier to join him than fight him bout it. He'd be gone lotsa days, and he'd get mad and hit me when I said anything he didn't like."

I can't tell you how many times I've heard different versions of that same story. A person is on fire for the Lord, and then the flame goes out because the world becomes stronger than the Kingdom of God. And then a pendulum path develops of being sober and going back to drugs and alcohol...again and again. Or flipping in and out of drug rehab centers ten times or more. Or being on a roller coaster of in and out of jail a dozen times or, for some, fifty.

The room became deathly silent before I asked Jasmine the defining question I ask every person I meet with.

"What are you going to do different this time, Jasmine, to end the cycle of drug addiction and crime that has you captured?"

She started crying again.

"I don't know, Chaplain, I guess it ain't in me to stay straight."

That's the conclusion I hoped she'd come to.

"That's right, Jasmine, there *is* nothing you can do to help yourself. You've proven that. It's time to try something different. You've accepted Jesus as your Savior, but you haven't accepted Him as your Lord and Master."

She brushed her hair back to buy time before she answered.

"How do I do that?"

Let's start with your getting to know Jesus. I want you to read the 1st chapter of the Gospel of John and then the 14th, 15th, and 16th chapters. We'll discuss them next week."

Chapter Five
Who's the real Jesus?

"But what about you?" He asked. "Who do you say I am?"

Matthew 16:15

Some people think Jesus Christ is a great moral teacher but reject His claim to be God. He's a good man, they say, but He's not the Savior of the world. He's simply a person who lived 2,000 years ago and met an untimely death on a Roman cross.

What do you believe about Jesus and what do you base it on? In other words, where do you get your information about who the real Jesus is?

Do you listen to your buddies over a cup of coffee or a beer or at a gathering of some sort? Do you read magazine articles or watch a famous person on TV talk about religion? How about some guy standing on a soapbox on a busy street corner?

It's not that there isn't any truth spoken in the above instances, but you need to find out for yourself. You need to learn about Jesus through the four gospels and epistles in the New Testament and through the Old Testament prophets.

If you're going to follow Jesus with all your heart and with all your soul, you need to know who He really is. Jasmine had a lot to learn about Jesus if she was to love and follow Him with her eyes wide open and her ears unplugged.

JASMINE'S STORY PART 2

The next week arrived on schedule, and Jasmine strolled into our meeting room like a little girl entering a fun house. Something wonderful had happened to her, but I didn't know what. Did someone post bond for her? Did she hear she'd get her kids back? Who *was* this new person sitting across from me?

"Who *are* you, Jasmine?"

My voice rose at the second word. I thought she'd ask me what I meant, but she didn't. She sat there with a big smile on her face and answered the question directly.

"I'm a child of God, and I love Jesus."

I sat back in my chair and folded my arms over my chest.

"Now where did that come from, Jasmine?" as if I didn't know.

The intensity of her smile could have melted steel.

"In what you said to read."

She opened her Bible to John 1:12.

Yet to all who received Him, to those who believed in His name, He gave the right to become children of God.

"It's right there," she said, like a woman showing someone her new engagement ring. "I'm a child of God."

At first I couldn't speak. I'm still amazed when God works through His Word such wonders to behold.

"You're indeed a child of God, and you've been one since the day you were saved, but now you know it in your spirit because the Bible says it."

I paused, and she sat there expecting me to say something more, which I did.

"You also said you love Jesus. Where did you find that?"

She opened her Bible to the three other chapters I had assigned her in the Gospel of John.

I saw John 14 highlighted in yellow and pencil notes in the margins. She wasn't just reading the Bible; she was inhaling it.

"Want me to read the yellow stuff?"

She pointed to the first three verses, as if she'd discovered a secret. Her voice trembled.

"I love Jesus cause of what He says here:"

Do not let your hearts be troubled. Trust in God; trust also in Me. In My Father's house are many rooms; if it were not so, I would have told you. I am going there to prepare a place for you. And if I go and prepare a place for you, I will come back and take you to be with me that you also may be where I am.

"Jesus is sayin He'll take me to Heaven when I die."

She sat back and waited for a response. She was spot on but couldn't have figured that out on her own, unschooled as she was with Scripture. The Holy Spirit gave her insights because she was reading with an open heart and a quiet mind. I rubbed the back of my neck with my right hand and asked her a big-league question.

"Do you think then that everything in life will be smooth sailing for you if you just trust in Jesus and His Father?"

I sat back and waited for her response, and waited some more. Finally she answered in a voice that stuttered.

"I-I'd like to b-believe that, but I don't see how my life is gonna be smooth s-sailing. I d-don't think I'll get my kids back, right away anyhow, and I m-might get sent to prison. I'm m-mixed up about that."

I felt sorry for her. That wonderful smile disappeared from her face, and a look of worry took its place. Even when we're saved, we still live in a fallen world where bad things happen to good people.

"Let's see what the Bible has to say. It's just a couple chapters away, in the last verse of Chapter 16:"

I have told you these things, so that in Me you may have peace. In this world you will have trouble. But take heart! I have overcome the world.

I was about to explain that verse, but she beat me to it.

"I didn't mark that one; I shoulda. Jesus doesn't say I won't get problems, but He says He'll be with me when they come. I get it now. Want me to read the other verses I marked?"

Jasmine was on a roll, and I didn't want to slow her down by trying to teach her anything. The Bible did a much better job.

"I marked the 6th verse in Chapter 14 cause it tells me Jesus died so I could come to the Father. He loved me first, and I love Him cause of that dyin stuff."

I am the way and the truth and the life. No one comes to the Father except through me.

"Jasmine," I said, "where did you find God first loved you?"

She gave me a blank look and shrugged her shoulders in an "I dunno" way.

"Always remember that the best commentary on the Bible is the Bible itself. The Holy Spirit revealed to you that God first loved you, but He backs it up in the first epistle of John."

I opened my Bible to 1 John 4:19 and read:

We love because He first loved us.

I'll never forget her look when I read that verse. It was like the look on a woman's face when her boyfriend tells her for the first time that he loves her.

Jasmine again flashed the smile that could melt steel.

"I got it now."

She turned to John 15:9 and read that verse she'd marked:

As the Father has loved Me, so have I loved you. Now remain in my love.

"Doesn't that verse say bout the same thing?"

"You've got it! Jasmine."

That day Jasmine's transformation began. We met many times after that, discussing mostly the Gospel of John. I've found John best shows who Jesus really is, why He came to Earth, and what He wants our relationship to Him to be. We also looked at other Scripture that deepened Jasmine's love for Jesus.

One day when we met, Jasmine said, "I've learned who Jesus really is, and I'm a leanin on Him like all get out. I know I'll never use again or be back in jail again cause I'm aligned with the Father."

It surprised me that she used the word *aligned.*

As if reading my mind, she said, "Bet you're wondering where I got the thing on aligned with the Father. I been reading a Bible called *The Message* cause it speaks in a way I understand. Do you know bout it?"

"I sure do. It's a Bible translated into everyday English by a Bible scholar named Eugene Peterson. I'm glad you're reading it. Anyway, where did you find the passage on alignment?"

Jasmine opened her Bible to John 5:24 and read aloud:

It's urgent that you listen carefully to this: Anyone here who believes what I am saying right now and aligns himself with the Father, who has in fact put me in charge, has at this very moment the real, lasting life and is no longer condemned to be an outsider. This person has taken a giant step from the world of the dead to the world of the living.

"Ain't that what you told me right at the git go? That I was standin in the wrong neighborhood. Well, I'm aligned with the Father now and stayin in the right neighborhood. And that's where I'm gonna stay when I get out."

I hope one day to run into her again and listen to her talk about Jesus, His great love for her, and her staying in God's neighborhood, which I believe with all my heart she'll do.

Chapter Six
Step 3: Put Jesus first in your heart.

So then, just as you received Christ Jesus as Lord, continue to live your lives in him.

Colossians 2:6

The phrase, *Ask Jesus into your heart* isn't in the Bible, but it mirrors what the Bible has to say about salvation, such as the verse above. What does it mean to ask Jesus into your heart? And if you do that, where do you put him?

AUSTIN'S STORY

Austin loved Jesus, but his alcoholism held him in a death lock that would not let him go. In a moment of deep despair he told me, "I'm just a hopeless drunk, Pat. I can't stop no matter what. I'm a loser." He was correct when he said he was a loser.

Over the course of a few years, Austin had lost his wife, children, job, house, truck, dog…and his self-esteem. I first met him two days after he'd pulled into the parking lot of a golf course, so drunk he didn't know where he was or how he got there. He passed out with the car running and didn't wake up until a couple hours later when he heard a tap, tap, tap on the window. It was a sheriff's deputy, who arrested him for DWI.

"Chaplain," he said then in jail, "Please help me. I can't stop drinking. I beg Jesus to keep me sober and He does for a while, but it doesn't last. Maybe I'm not worth His attention."

The Holy Spirit nudged me to offer Austin guidance after he said goodbye to the jail in a couple of days.

"Would you like to keep meeting with me, Austin?"

His head came up, and there was a gleam of hope that came into his eyes, something I hadn't seen before then.

"Definitely, that's what I need. Will you do that for me?"

The hint of a smile lifted his lips from the downward slouch that appeared painted on his face with indelible ink. That was the start of many meetings between us after his release.

I've come to understand the ruthless power of an addiction through Austin. We studied Scripture together. We prayed together. He'd grow in Christ, fall back to drinking, and then get up again and promise to never touch another drop.

After two years of this pattern, I wondered if it were possible that a person like Austin could be so controlled by an addiction that he'd die with it. Was he really a hopeless drunk? Could a person be redeemed in the Spirit and remain sick in the body? Was alcoholism like cancer – some people can be healed of it but most aren't and eventually die?

Romans 8:28 says, *And we know that in all things God works for the good of those who love him, who have been called according to his purpose.* How did that apply to Austin?

I confessed to God one morning that I had nothing to offer Austin that made a lasting difference. What the Holy Spirit revealed to me then not only turned the tide for Austin but for many others since.

It's hard to explain how the Lord speaks to anyone, but these words came into my mind, in a fuzzy kind of way, "No, you can't, but I can." Then, the Holy Spirit showed me this picture:

In a snap of the fingers, I vividly understood its meaning and thanked God for bringing it to light. I met with Austin later that afternoon.

"What are we going to do with you?" I asked Austin in the conference room of the coffee shop where we regularly met.

He hung his head in shame. "I don't know, Pat. Nothing I do works. I appreciate you trying to help, but it doesn't last. Even Jesus can't help me. I guess I'm just a loser in life."

"Would you like to be a winner, Austin?"

"Definitely! I want to be a winner, for sure. But I can't find a way. I'm a born-again believer but that doesn't seem to help."

"What do you think God's will is for you?" I asked.

"Not be a drunk, I guess, but why can't I stop then?"

"Of course He wants you to stop drinking, but that's not the starting point. He wants a personal relationship with you on His terms. That's His underlying will."

Austin sniffled and spoke out of years of frustration.

"If I'm a believer, Pat, aren't I living in God's will? So why can't I stop drinking?"

At this point, Austin broke down and said no more. I prayed silently for the Holy Spirit to guide me.

"When you were saved, Austin, did you invite Jesus into your heart?"

He answered quickly, "Definitely. I used those very words."

"Can you tell me what it means to invite Jesus into your heart, Austin?"

"What do you mean, Pat?"

"I mean, what exactly is your heart and how do you invite Jesus into it?"

I could tell he didn't expect that question by his body language. He shrugged his shoulders and his eyes crossed.

"I don't think we're talking about the heart that pumps blood, are we?" I shook my head to the rhythm of a no. "I guess I don't know then; I've never thought about it."

His answer didn't surprise me. We often use words and phrases that have been used over and over, without having a mental grasp of what they really mean.

"The Bible's always the best place to start when we want to understand spiritual things," I began, "Let's look at two verses to give us a clue."

Blessed are the pure in heart for they will see God.
Matthew 5:8

A good man brings good things out of the good stored up in his heart, and an evil man brings evil things out of the evil stored up in his heart.
Luke 6:45

"First of all, the heart in Scripture is a metaphor rather than an actual thing like our body, soul, or spirit."

"What's a metaphor, Pat?"

"A metaphor is something familiar used to represent something that's hard to understand. Does that make sense?"

"Definitely. So what does the heart represent?"

"That's the question of the day, Austin. It's an invisible room deep within us that holds what's most important to us and reflects our deepest feelings and beliefs. It's like a lock box where we tuck away what we value most. Make sense?"

Matt's eyes shone with the light of understanding and his shoulders were steady.

"Definitely. Would the love of Jesus be in my heart?"

I nodded yes, with a wink, "It would be if you invited Jesus into your heart."

"So that's what it means to invite Jesus into my heart – to ask Him to live where I store my most important things?"

Well, he had part of it. His next statement bore witness to the missing piece. His laughter turned to frustration.

"But, Pat, if I've got Jesus in my heart, why can't I stop drinking. I read the Bible every day and pray every day. I love Jesus and try to walk with Him. What else do I need to do?"

I had an unearthly sense of confidence that the Holy Spirit was guiding me in this discussion.

"Yes, Austin, I believe you have Jesus in your heart, but you have Him in the wrong place."

He gave me one of those *huh* looks.

I arose from my chair and drew on the board the two hearts the Holy Spirit had shown me. Then I turned around.

"The first heart is you going your own way and asking Jesus to follow after you and help you out when you need Him."

I paused to catch my breath before lowering the boom.

"You're treating Jesus like a little puppy dog who follows you to do your bidding. 'Jesus, come on, help me with my drinking. Jesus, keep me sober. Jesus, help me get back with my girlfriend and help me find a job. (At this point I whistled like you would for a puppy dog.) Come on Jesus, come on buddy.'"

Austin looked confused.

"What's wrong with that? Isn't Jesus supposed help us in our troubles?"

"That's not the way it works with Jesus, Austin. You need to let Him lead and you follow. He knows the road better than you do. He knows where He wants you to go, and you don't."

Austin was focused on the first heart, as if the second didn't exist.

"So I'm a loser then, just a hopeless drunk?"

He closed his eyes and his head dropped down until it was a foot from the surface of the table.

"Yes, you're a loser when you're in the lead and going your own way with Jesus trailing after you.

"The second heart is the way God wants you to live – putting Jesus in front of you and following Him where He wants you to go. That's the way of a winner!

"In the first drawing, you say, 'Austin is most important.' In the second one you say, 'Jesus is most important.'"

Austin blurted out in excitement, "I think I've got it!"

The Holy Spirit led me in what next to say.

"Instead of pleading, 'Jesus help me with my drinking,' say, 'Jesus, I want to follow You wherever You go.' Do you think Jesus would lead you into a bar you're walking past?"

Austin laughed. "No way! And if I'm reaching for a bottle of vodka in my apartment, what do I do?"

You may think I'd have told him he shouldn't have a bottle of vodka there in the first place, but I didn't because that wasn't the right answer. He'd just go out and buy another bottle anyway. No, The Holy Spirit had him, and I wasn't going to get in the way with impractical advice.

"Ask Jesus if he'd like to sit with you and have a double?"

Austin laughed again. "No way He'd want to do that!"

"Then you don't either. The two of you are a team on the road of your life, but you have to let Him lead. You follow a half step behind, close enough to talk with Him but letting there be no doubt who's leading, who's following, and who's greater and who's lesser."

Austin banged his hand on the table.

"I'll do it. No more puppy-dog Jesus. I'll follow Him into Hell if that's what He wants."

"I don't think He'd take you there, Austin, but maybe through a Hell on earth."

"Definitely! that's what I meant."

Austin now follows Jesus past bars and drinks mineral water with Him and asks himself at every step: "Would Jesus do this with me?" or "What would Jesus have me do here?" I ask myself those two questions as well.

Chapter Seven
Be filled with more of God than of you.

He must become greater; I must become less.

John 3:30

In a syndicated cartoon strip popular from 1948 to 1975, a character named Pogo said to his friend the porcupine, "We have met the enemy and he is us." Truer words were never spoken.

There can only be one God in our lives; and if it isn't the Lord God Almighty, then who or what is it? Our own proud and self-seeking individuality is enemy-number-one. Second place among the enemies list is a toss-up. A young man whom I've mentored for several years has faced more than his share.

TANNER'S STORY

Just when I thought I had a handle on Tanner, he'd surprise me by flying off to California on a sudden impulse and drinking and drugging himself into a stupor. Then he'd return home with a truckload of remorse, regret, and repentance.

Tanner was a passionate Christian. But, for the life of me, I couldn't figure out what caused him to be on fire for the Lord one day and passed out and sailing off the road into a corn field the next evening.

Tanner had been in addiction rehab 14 times: seven inpatient and seven outpatient. He'd tried to commit suicide five times, feeling the world would be better off without him. His father had beaten his mother while little Tanner peeked out the door of the bathroom, then left the house to never come back. Trauma like that leaves deep wounds in the soul of a little boy that aren't easily healed when he becomes a young man.

Tanner's mother tried to raise him and his two sisters as best she could, but she had her own issues and sought love in all the wrong places. Dysfunctional defined how their home worked.

Tanner's negative home life and less-than-wholesome experiences made him ill-equipped to make good choices. By the time he stepped into his 13th birthday, he hung around other boys who had painful lives or otherwise lived on the edge of society. He started using drugs that year and alcohol a year later. When high or drunk, his life seemed bearable. Tanner was shy, but his questionable friends accepted him just the way he was. The more he used or drank, the more outgoing he became.

I first met Tanner at a McDonald's and listened to his sad story. When we got together next, it was more give and take. Tanner never showed for our third meeting. I had no idea where he'd gone until he called from a Minneapolis hospital.

He'd been living out of his car for two weeks, drinking and taking drugs until he'd pass out. His mother and sister had found him standing on a railroad track, waiting for a train to pulverize him. They're the ones who brought him to the hospital.

"Pat, I've hit rock bottom. I'm ready to turn my life around. For sure I'm ready. No fooling around this time."

I can't believe what I said next. I should've been supportive of his promise to turn his life around, but the Holy Spirit knew what he needed – shock treatment.

"Tanner, you're not going to turn your life around. You don't have what it takes. Let me tell you what's going to happen. You'll get out of that hospital in a week. A few days later, you'll start using again, and you'll start thinking the world would be better off without you. One day you'll overdose and die or hang yourself or be run over by a train. Then you'll find yourself in Hell for all eternity. That's what's going to happen to you."

I thought our connection might have been lost because I couldn't hear anything on the other end of the line.

"Are you still there, Tanner? Did you hear what I said?"

"Yah. I'm here and heard what you said. I'm just kinda scared stiff. I don't know what to say. It sounds awful what you said. What hope is there for me then? I might as well kill myself right now and be done with it."

I was deeply disturbed by his talking about suicide. Had I been too hard on him? Did I push him over the edge? Why did I say what I did? The Holy Spirit got me into this. I prayed He would show me what to say next, and He did.

"You need to meet the real Jesus, Tanner, not just thoughts about Him you have in your mind. Go into your room, open your Bible, and ask to meet Jesus."

The next morning he called me all excited and told me about his encounter the previous evening.

"It's for sure hard to explain. I didn't see Jesus standing before me or hear Him out loud, but I knew it was Him.

"It's like He was in my mind but not in my mind, you know what I mean? It was like a secret voice, you know, a whisper. And that whisper said, 'It will be all right, son.' I felt God like grabbing me. And I cried without tears."

Tanner's life turned on a dime that day – from the darkness of the world to the light of Jesus Christ and the Kingdom of God. Now, becoming a born-again Christian is one thing, but sustaining that life is something else entirely. When I visited him in the hospital, we had a long discussion.

"Tanner, you've repented of your sins and have accepted Jesus as your Savior and Lord, but now you need to work out your salvation."

"What do you mean work out my salvation, Pat?"

"I mean you need to let the Holy Spirit and others increase your knowledge about God and bolster your faith to become the mature Christian God wants you to be."

"Such as?"

"If it's possible, I'd suggest staying at a Christian residential rehabilitation center like Minnesota Teen Challenge, Metro Hope in Minneapolis, the Salvation Army, or Next Chapter in Rochester. In those places, you'll get a firm foundation in Biblical study and prayer and what it means to live out your life in the light of Christ's kingdom. Plus, you'll be surrounded by fellow Christians struggling with the same issues you have.

"If that won't work for you, you need to find at least one strong believer who can guide you on how to navigate the Christian walk and be an accountability partner for you. A mentor so to speak."

Tanner looked at me with eyes that scanned my soul.

"Could you be that person for me, Pat?"

"I'm willing to do that, Tanner, but if you can, a residential program would be best for you. Then I can mentor you when you graduate."

"Sounds great, Pat. Can I have time to think it over?"

"Of course."

After being released from the hospital, Tanner went to the Minneapolis Adult and Teen Challenge for 13 months where he became grounded in who the real Jesus is and how to follow Him from dawn to dusk.

When he left there, he landed a job driving a parts store delivery truck. For a year, he attended two church services each Sunday and attended Celebrate Recovery meetings regularly. He had an AA Sponsor and got up two hours early every morning for Scripture reading and prayer. While driving, he only listened to Christian radio stations.

Tanner and I talked twice a week and met in person at least once a month. I was impressed with his passion for Jesus.

I wish that were the end of Tanner's story. One afternoon, he called and announced he'd started his own lawn maintenance business on weekends. I didn't see the red flag at the time.

He soon had more jobs than he could handle. He asked his company if he could switch to four-day weeks. They agreed but only if he worked the same number of hours.

He drove the delivery truck 10 to 12 hours a day and took care of lawns three days a week. Busyness became the enemy that drew him away from Jesus. Tanner no longer had the energy to get up two hours early for prayer and Scripture reading. He couldn't make his Celebrate Recovery meetings and didn't have time for AA meetings or for meeting with his sponsor. He skipped church on Sundays and withdrew from all meaningful Christian relationships. And he listened to rock music in his work truck.

In short, Tanner stopped doing the right things and lost touch with his core beliefs and his faith. He was a different Tanner than the one who'd been saved in the hospital.

The diagram below shows what happened to him:

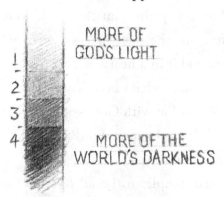

Anything that takes the rightful place of God in our lives is darkness, but that doesn't mean we're standing in either pure darkness or perfect light all the time. It's more of a continuum of light and darkness based on whether we're more in the Kingdom of God or more in the world at any given point in time.

Number **1** defined Tanner after being born-again in a Minneapolis hospital and during 13 months at Adult and Teen Challenge. God took up 80% of his life.

Number **2** represented Tanner when he left Adult and Teen Challenge and started working for the parts store. A job, car problems, and the standard necessities of food, shelter and clothing became distractions to following Jesus. Life in general became an enemy. Mature Christ-followers have learned to incorporate God into even the most common things of their lives, but Tanner was a few hundred miles away from being one of them.

Number **3** described Tanner when he started the his lawn maintenance business. Suddenly he was packing ten pounds of busyness into a five-pound bag. Those extra five pounds were an enemy to his staying near Jesus.

Number **4** became Tyler's settling point within four weeks of the overstuffed bag, and Jesus was nowhere to be found. He started using again so heavily that he blacked out three times driving his car. His addiction became his enemy with a vengeance. After the third time, he realized he needed to re-acquaint himself with Jesus or he'd end up dead.

When I drew out the *more of God, more of the world* chart to Tanner, he understood it in a heartbeat.

"For sure, Pat, that's what's been happening to me. It's, like, the story of my life. When I'm with God, good things happen. When I'm not with God, bad things happen. It's that simple. I need to be all-out for God. That's all there is to it."

It really is that simple: to be all out for God is the unfailing prerequisite of eternal success. For me, to be in the Lord's presence requires that I not be in my own presence as much as I'm in His presence. The chart I showed Tanner painted a picture of what he didn't understand with just words.

"What are you going to do now, Tanner, now that you realize the life you're living doesn't work?"

"What do you think I should do, Pat?"

"I think you need to reacquaint yourself with the real Jesus. Why don't you pray and let me know what appears."

I didn't tell Tanner what to do because that would be my choice, not his. He needed to claim ownership.

Tanner signed up for a stay at a Christian-based residential facility, where he had a safe place to live while he worked in a factory nearby. From there he went to a trade school and is now working as a locksmith in the Minneapolis area. He's sober, but he tells me it's not easy. Temptations to use drugs and drink bombard him like bats out of you know where. But he combats them by doing what he needs to do to stay near Jesus.

THE POWER OF ADDICTIONS

There are lies behind every addiction:

I can't live without this. I need drugs to deal with stress, pain, and all the other problems I have. I can't imagine my life without alcohol. I'm helpless to quit my addiction. It's the only pleasure and comfort I have in life.

These lies reflect the darkness of this fallen world. A small percentage of addicts can turn their lives around by the power of their wills. Most can't. Jesus Christ is the Truth and the Light that can lead you out of darkness, if you let Him.

So, does a flash of lightning turn your darkness into light in the twinkling of an eye? That's not the usual pattern. It's more of a journey than a moment in time, and direction is more important than perfection. What's most important is an intent to follow Jesus and seek Him with all your heart.

You have the time in jail or a rehab facility to concentrate on Scripture reading, prayer, Bible studies, and Christian fellowship. You may think you're well equipped, but if you don't walk closely behind Jesus when you leave, you'll lose your way again. But how do you do that unless you have a plan?

What I'm going to tell you next is where that plan comes from and what's in it.

Chapter Eight
Step 4: Plan to read the Bible daily.

*For I know the plans I have for you, declares the LORD, plans
to prosper you and not to harm you, plans to give you hope
and a future. Then you will call on me and come and pray
to me, and I will listen to you. You will seek me and find me
when you seek me with all your heart.*

Jeremiah 29:11-13

Mike Tyson, the former heavyweight boxing champion of the
world, once proclaimed, "Everybody has a plan until they get punched
in the mouth." Robert Burns, a Scottish poet, wrote that the best laid
plans of men often go astray.

We can sketch out well-meaning plans of our own, but chronic
health issues, the death of a loved one, or the loss of a job can become
a punch in the mouth. And the best laid plans can go astray when
troubles and problems come door knocking.

This is especially true for addicts who can't stop drinking or using
no matter how well-intentioned their plans are to quit. Or inmates
who plan to never return to jail but do, over and over. Or for those in
dark places who can't find the light on their own.

The Jeremiah passage above tells us we need to pay attention to
God's plans, not our own. But how do we go about the seeking and
finding?

SCOTT'S STORY PART 1

I met with Scott in the conference room of a coffee shop in Buffalo, the day after he left addiction rehab for the seventh time. After some chit chat, I posed my usual question.

"Scott, what're you going to do different this time than the other six times that all ended in failure to stay sober?"

He shrugged his shoulders. "I don't know."

I shrugged my shoulders to imitate his gesture. "So you're just going to dum de dum your way through life?"

It wasn't meant to be a kind remark, and he didn't take it as such. He suddenly sat straight up as if he'd stuck his finger in a power socket and spoke with the voice of a person whose face had just been slapped.

"What do you mean dum de dum my way through life?"

Well, I'd caught his attention, which was my intent, but I needed to quickly show him I meant no harm. My voice softened.

"I mean you just let your life go on without a plan. You're saved and know the truth of the Bible, but you don't act on it."

No doubt, Scott's answer came from all the advice he'd heard in rehab about how to stay sober.

"Yah, sure, I know. Like plan to avoid all my friends and move to another state and start over? That's really cool. Maybe I should plan to move to China where I won't know anyone? How about I become a missionary there?"

I didn't say anything. Scott rambled on with his sarcastic collection of preposterous choices he could make to stay off drugs, ending up with being a hermit in the Himalayas.

"Why do I have to make tough choices? Why doesn't God just take away my addiction? That's what I pray for."

I saw Scott turn his head to the door and heard his legs shuffle under the table, as if he were about to get up and leave.

My Bible sat on the left corner of the table. I grabbed it quick as a wink and flipped it to two verses I live by.

"I'm not going to give you any of that advice, Scott. I've found that just saying no to alcohol or drugs works about as well as saying no to food when you're starving. Some people can stop using by force of will; most can't.

"And avoiding the friends who may be the only ones there for you can leave you walking the streets by yourself.

"What you really need to do is something different than anything you've done before. Albert Einstein said that doing the same things over and over and expecting different results is the definition of insanity."

Scott kind of laughed.

"You've heard what the world has to say about staying sober. Let's hear what God's plan is."

He watched me hard as I spoke in the hush-hush voice of a person telling secrets.

Come near to God and He will come near to you.

James 4:8

Remain in Me, and I will remain in you.

John 15:4

Scott stopped peeking at the door and looked fixedly at me. I switched back to my normal voice and continued.

"You see, Scott, the Bible says you make the first move, not God. He doesn't usually come crashing into your life unannounced. You must come near to Him and remain there. You came to Him when you asked Him to save you and you stayed near Him during your three-month stay at Adult and Teen Challenge. Then you left Jesus standing on the north side of your life path as you headed south.

"You don't have a plan for how to stay sober. Don't you see that not having a plan *is* a plan in itself? And so you dum de dum your way through life."

I figured I'd gone far enough and stopped talking. I took a sip of coffee and prayed that Scott would ask the question I hoped he'd ask, and he did, right on cue.

"You nailed me, Pat. I hear what you're saying. So what does a plan look like? I don't want to dum de dum my way through life or whatever you call it. I want to stay sober. I want to be a good husband and father. I want to keep a job and be a good provider. If I don't make it this time, my wife said she'll leave me and take the kids and go live with her parents."

I saw a tear in his eye.

"You hadn't told me that before, Scott. Now you really need to have a plan."

By the look on his face, I'd hit him right between the eyes.

"Absolutely, but how do I do a plan? Will you help me do one?"

"Do you mean will I help you develop a plan? The answer to that is a no."

He looked like a little boy who'd just been told he couldn't go to the birthday party of his best friend.

"Why not? You said you wanted to help me."

I put my elbows on the table, leaned over, and looked him straight in the eyes.

"Because if I come up with a plan for you, it'll be my plan. And if you come up with a plan, it'll be your plan. Neither one is good enough. How about we look in the Bible to see what plan God has in mind for your life? I'll help you with that."

I saw a sigh of relief on his face.

"You had me going there sure thing, Pat. I thought maybe you'd pick up and go."

"I wouldn't do that, Scott. I'm in this for the long haul. But I want you to get your help from the Lord, not me. I'm only His messenger. Are you ready to let the Holy Spirit lay out a plan for you?"

Scott's face took on a determined look. He didn't smile.

"Absolutely."

I wanted Scott to be part of the process, so I didn't just reveal the plan from Scripture. I asked him questions instead.

"Okay, Scott, if you want to stay near Jesus, you want to know all about Him. And where might you find that?"

He didn't want to take the chance he might be wrong, so his answer came out more like a question.

"In the Bible?"

"Exactly. Let's look there and see what we find."

"Let's do it," he said, as if he were now in control. "Let's find it in the Bible."

"Sounds good to me, Scott. Turn to 2 Timothy 3:16 and read it out loud."

He opened his Bible, which looked like it had been taken out of the box it came in that very morning:

All Scripture is God-breathed and is useful for teaching, rebuking, correcting, and training in righteousness.

"What do you think that means, Scott?'

He didn't hesitate.

"It means the Bible is God's book and teaches us right from wrong and things like that."

"Great answer, but how about the word *righteousness*? What do you think that suggests?"

He gave the answer I thought he'd give.

"It means the Bible will train me to do right things, right?"

His voice was confident, but he'd missed the main meaning. I didn't want to let the air out of his balloon, so I used a by-the-way manner of speaking.

"That's part of it, Scott, but the word means something else as well. It means to be in right standing with God, which means doing things His way instead of your own way. That's a good reason why you should read the Bible all the time – to find out what His way is and head in that direction."

He nodded his head.

"Neat. That makes sense. So how often is all the time?"

I was ready for that question and pulled an Amplified Old Testament out of my briefcase, opened it up to Joshua 1:8, and read. I wanted to use the Amplified version because of its expanded translation of the original Hebrew:

> This Book of the Law shall not depart from your mouth, but you shall read [and meditate on] it day and night, so that you may be careful to do [everything] in accordance with all that is written in it; for then you will make your way prosperous, and then you will be successful.

"Does that answer your question? All the time isn't specific enough. Day and night gives a better guideline. Or, how about we just say daily?

"So that's the plan, Pat, to read the Bible daily? And meditate means to think over what I'm reading?"

"That's the plan, Scott. Indeed, that's the plan."

"But where do I start, Pat. I mean like do I start at the beginning of the Bible and go to the end?"

"I'd suggest you start with the Gospel of John in the New Testament and Genesis in the Old, reading back and forth between the two of them. Then read through Matthew, Mark, and Luke; and Exodus and the Psalms in the Old Testament, in the same back and forth manner. Then we can discuss where to go after that. If you google *Read through the Bible in a year*, you'll find all sorts of plans.

"You can have two different times to study Scripture – one for the New Testament and one for the Old."

"What? How am I going to find time to do that? I've got a job and a family you know."

"There'll never be the time to read Scripture if you try to shoehorn it into your daily life. You need to take time from something else."

"Like what?"

"What time does your family get up in the morning?"

"About 7 O'clock."

"Then you get up at 6:00 and spend an hour in prayer and studying John and the other three gospels."

"What do you do after supper?"

"I watch TV until I go to bed. It relaxes me."

"Take a half hour from your TV watching and read from Genesis, Exodus, and Psalms."

"But some of my favorite programs are back to back."

"Tape them and watch them later. You'll save 15 minutes just by skipping the commercials. Taping two programs will give you the half hour you need."

"Neat. I never thought of that. I can do that."

It's interesting that Scott had his hand on the Bible he brought when he made that promise. I didn't make a comment. He knew what he meant by it.

"No matter what else you do, just reading the Bible according to a plan is one of the most important things you can do, if not *the* most important.

"But [followed by a long pause], you don't want to read the Bible like a magazine or newspaper. God speaks to us through His word, and you want to listen closely. And that's not the end of it. You also want to discover the meaning of what you're reading as it applies to your own life and put it into practice."

Scott sat with his lips parted but no words came out at first. Finally he spoke.

"That's too much coming at me all at once, Pat. I feel buried."

"I can understand that, Scott. Let me give you an example from everyday life to see if that helps sort it out."

"Okay. Go for it."

"Do you remember when you got your driver's license in high school?"

Absolutely. Then I could go places without having to hound my parents for a ride."

"Did someone just hand you the driver's license one day?"

"Fat chance. I learned the rules of the road in a manual I picked up at the license place downtown."

"Did you just read through it once?"

"Try ten times. I studied it until I knew everything in it because I had to take a written test, which I aced."

"And then they gave you your driver's license?"

"Not quite. I had to pass a driving test too, you know, driving a car with a license officer checking me out."

"Did you take that test as soon as you passed the written test?"

"Absolutely not. I had to practice like crazy with a driving instructor until she told me I was ready for the test. And when I aced that test, I got my driver's license."

I smiled.

"That's the way it is with reading the Bible, Scott. It's your driver's manual. You don't want to just read through the Bible. You want to study it as if you're going to take an exam.

"Then you want to practice applying it to your life like you practiced driving a car. Then and only then can you be confident that you know where you're going in the Kingdom of God and how to get there. In effect, the Bible is your roadmap. Does it make sense now?"

"Absolutely. Now it makes sense, but how do I do that? Do I just read through it over and over like a driver's manual?" He paused. "Good gravy, I must really seem stupid when it comes to all this stuff."

"You're not stupid, Scott, not at all. You're just uninformed. My job is to inform you. I'd suggest you buy a Study Bible to help with the studying part of it."

"My wife has one of those, but it's for women."

"You can find a good Study Bible for everyone or just for men in a Christian bookstore or online, like on Amazon."

"Okay, I can do that."

His hand remained on his Bible.

"Anything more? You said I shouldn't be reading stuff in the Bible like reading a magazine. How should I read it?"

"Well, you should be thinking about what you're reading and praying on it."

"Say again? What's that mean?"

"You know, Scott, I think it would be better to show you what I mean instead of telling you, okay?"

"Sure. Go for it."

"Please turn to the Gospel of John and read the first two verses of the first chapter:"

In the beginning was the Word, and the Word was with God, and the Word was God. He was with God in the beginning.

"*The Word* is Jesus Christ in this passage, and Jesus was both with God and always was God right from the beginning. So when you pray to Jesus, you're automatically praying to God. In John 10:30, Jesus says, *I and the Father are one.* This is the mystery of the trinity that can't be adequately explained in our three-dimensional world."

I paused for effect. Scott was motionless, as if he were in a spell of some kind.

"Here's one way you could think about and pray about these two verses."

Lord Jesus, thank You for being the Word and for coming down on earth to die for our sins. You are a great God. You are a mighty God. I know I can't understand You completely, but it gives me great hope just to know that You're God. I love You Jesus for who You are and what You did for me, my God and my Savior.

The look on Scott's face told me I'd gotten through.

"Wow! I never would of thought about doing something like that. How about another example?"

"Okay. Turn farther ahead in John to the 14th chapter and read verses 15 and 16:"

If you love me, you will obey what I command. And I will ask the Father, and He will give you another Counselor to be with you forever – the Spirit of truth.

When Scott finished reading he asked, "How do I know what Jesus commands?" Before I could say anything, he answered his own question. "Don't say it."

"Don't say what?"

"Say I'll find it in the Bible."

"OK, I won't say it, but you're right. For example, in more than one place, Scripture says to *Love the Lord your God with all your heart and with all your soul and with all your mind and with all your strength.*

"Jesus calls that the most important commandment.

"With this in mind, let's look at John 14:15-16 and I'll give you an example of how to think about this and pray it:"

> *Lord Jesus, I love You and want to obey Your commands. I want to learn all of them from Your Word. I thank You for sending the Holy Spirit to teach me truth. I want to know the truth about You, and I'm going to read about You and the Father every day from now on. But I know I can't do it on my own, so I'll depend on the Holy Spirit to show me what to read and what it means.*

Scott sat there with a furrowed brow and a determined face, as if translating my prayer into his own language.

"Pat, can I give it a try with a verse I've highlighted because it's talking right at me – John 14:1."

> *Do not let your hearts be troubled. Trust in God; trust also in Me.*

"That's a great verse, Scott. I'm glad you highlighted it. Give it a try."

> *Father God, my heart is troubled because of my addiction and things like that, and it's messed me up and harmed*

my family. I can't forgive myself, but I know You can. I've tried and tried to stop using and drinking but it's no good. I give up. I'm turning it all over to You, Father God, because I trust You and I trust Jesus. I believe You can handle it. I can't. I don't pray this on my own, Father God, but in Jesus' name.

He stopped, and I sat there amazed. He'd just prayed that Scripture as if he'd been handed a script by the Holy Spirit. I sat silent and motionless, feeling like I was on holy ground. It took me the better part of a minute to respond.

"Scott, I don't know what to say. That was a great prayer that you put in your own language. I'm impressed, and I believe God is very pleased with you as well."

He nodded in agreement as we got up and left the coffee shop to walk the streets of life, and Scott with a new resolve to read the Bible daily in a meaningful way.

Chapter Nine
Step 5: Plan to pray continually.

But Jesus often withdrew to lonely places and prayed.

Luke 5:16

Nearly half of Americans pray every day, according to a Lifeway Research survey. As for what they're praying for:

- 82 percent pray for friends and family.

- 74 percent pray for their own needs and difficulties.

- 42 percent pray for their own sins.

- 38 percent pray for those stricken by natural disasters.

- About 20 percent pray to win the lottery, for no one to find out about a bad thing they did, for God to avenge someone who hurt them or a loved one, or for their favorite team to win a game.

- About 10 percent pray for bad things to happen to bad people, to not get caught speeding, or to find a parking spot.

Is this all there is to prayer? Is this how Jesus taught His disciples to pray? The real questions that need answering involve why we pray, how, and where?

SCOTT'S STORY PART 2

Scott and I met in the same coffee shop conference room. I walked over to the whiteboard on the wall and wrote down *Read the Bible Daily* and put a 1 in front of it.

"What do you think number 2 might be, Scott?"

"You talked last week about reading the Bible daily and that the next one would make up the most important two or the big two or something like that. I *prayed* about it all week."

Scott laughed at his cleverness.

I turned back to the board, wrote the number 2, and put *Pray Continually* after it. Scott chuckled with delight.

"That's a good guess, Pat. I even know where you found that pray continually verse."

He opened his freshly worn Bible to 1 Thessalonians 5:17 and read that verse and the ones before and after:

> *[16]Rejoice always,[17] pray continually,[18] give thanks in all circumstances; for this is God's will for you in Christ Jesus.*

"That's it, Pat, right?" I nodded. "But that praying continually's got me. I can hardly go more than 15 minutes before I run out of people and stuff to pray about."

"That's what we're going to talk about today, Scott. Pay special attention to the verse after 17. Giving thanks in all circumstances is one way to pray continually."

"For sure, Pat, but there's gotta be more to praying continually than just that. Something else, you know."

"In the 5th chapter of Matthew, Jesus gives the disciples what we call The Lord's Prayer. Do you know that prayer?"

Scott nodded his head.

"I used to have the same problem with praying as you do. I'd get through lifting up my family and friends and people with health issues and problems I was having in less than a half hour. And then I'd do the same thing the next morning. 'There has to be more to praying than this,' I pleaded one morning.

"The next Sunday, a visiting missionary spoke at our church about using the Lord's Prayer as an outline of prayer. When she finished speaking, I thought to myself, 'That's the answer to my request of God last Tuesday.'"

I stopped there and sipped from my coffee mug on the table. I could tell Scott expected me to continue on, but I said nothing.

"Hey, Pat, are you going to tell me what she said?"

Now I had him hooked.

"What if I told you that you could pray the Lord's Prayer once through for at least an hour? And what if I told you that you could pray it again later in the day with different thoughts and words? And what if I told you that you could pray one part of it to start the day and another part driving to work and another part during a quiet time in your office?"

"I'd say you know something I don't."

"Well, Scott, why don't I tell you what I know?"

"Sounds good," he said, as he watched me walk to the board.

I grabbed a marker and drew the side of a house.

"This is a house of prayer and these seven boards, nailed to vertical studs behind them, make up the framework."

"I know construction," Scott said. "But what's this got to do with the Lord's Prayer?"

"Patience, my friend. Let me finish."

Without delay, I wrote the petitions of the Lord's prayer on the boards, which you'll find at the top of the next page:

```
OUR FATHER WHO ART IN HEAVEN

HALLOWED BE THY NAME

THY KINGDOM COME

THY WILL BE DONE ON EARTH AS IN HEAVEN

GIVE US THIS DAY OUR DAILY BREAD

AND FORGIVE US OUR SINS AS WE FORGIVE

AND LEAD US NOT INTO TEMPTATION
```

Scott had a notebook open during the five minutes it took me to complete the framework. I could see him copying down the chart, only occasionally picking up his coffee mug for a sip.

"Each of these seven boards represents one petition of the Lord's prayer. The top one is called *Our Father Who Art in Heaven.*"

With that, I moved from the board to the table and sat down. Scott lifted his coffee mug with his pen still in hand and nearly spilled it. We both laughed.

"Pat, I got a feeling this will fill our two hours today."

"That's right, Scott. I just hope we can get through all of it."

I double-gulped my coffee before explaining the first board.

"*Our Father Who Art in Heaven* is our cue to declare that God is far above us, and His ways are greater than our ways, and His thoughts greater than our thoughts. We can also declare that Jesus is our King, who is also in heaven but within us through the power of the Holy Spirit, and that at His name every knee will bow and every tongue will acknowledge God. This is also a good place to promise that we'll go God's way instead of our own way."

Scott's eyes lit up like neon lights. He had it.

"That's cool. You use the words of the Lord's prayer as hints of what to pray about. It doesn't have to be praying about yourself or others all the time."

He started writing furiously in his notebook.

"You're right again. The first four petitions of the Lord's prayer are about Him and the last three are about ourselves."

The Holy Spirit joined the conversation as we discussed another ten ways we could pray about our Father in Heaven, ending with thanking Him for being our God and for creating us in His image and likeness. It was time for the next board –*Hallowed be Thy name.*

"What do you think the second one means, Scott?"

He understood the process and didn't hesitate.

"I imagine it means this is where we praise God and worship Him, right, like at the beginning of a church service? And we'd praise and worship Jesus too, right?"

"Right again."

I noticed that Scott was using a standard outline format to take down what we discussed:

1. Our Father who art in Heaven.
    a. God far above us, His ways greater than ours.
    b. Jesus our King, in Heaven and within us by H.S.
    [The outline went all the way to n.]
2. Hallowed be Thy name – praise and worship.
    a. Like at beginning of church service.

"Where did you learn to outline like that, Scott?"

"I had a college professor who taught us how to take notes. Without that, there's no way we could've kept up with him."

We made it to j on the outline before Scott said, "I think I got this one, Pat. We could spend an hour here, but I'm hoping to make it to the 7th board."

"Okay. How about *Thy kingdom come*? What ideas do you have on that?"

He thought before answering.

"Does that mean about when Jesus comes again at the end of time, like it says in the Bible?"

"That's part of it, Scott. What do you think other parts are?"

His blank look informed me his mind was blank as well.

"The Kingdom of God has come to you, right?"

"Right."

"You can thank God for dying on the cross so His kingdom could come to you."

"Absolutely."

"Do you have friends or family members who aren't saved?"

"Absolutely, lots of them."

"Then you can pray for The Kingdom of God to come to them, and ask what you could do to help that happen."

"That's probably better than asking God to heal their sicknesses and take care of their problems, right?"

"Exactly. What good is health in this life if eternal damnation is waiting on the other side of the curtain?"

The ink was being deposited on his notebook paper in gallons – or so it seemed.

"Cool, Pat. I got it. Let's move on."

"We're not done with this board, Scott. There's one more thing you can add to your outline."

"Okay, what's missing?"

"Something you can really sink your teeth into during prayer."

He didn't need to say anything. The look of eagerness on his face told me he was tuned in and ready to take notes.

"Christ-followers aren't storm troopers marching on their own. They're attached to the Army of the Lord to help advance the Kingdom of God on Earth while their hearts still beat.

"This is the place where you ask God what you can do to advance His kingdom today and tomorrow. Who can you talk to? Who can you disciple? Who can you serve? This is the part of the Lord's prayer that moved me to become a chaplain in the Wright County Jail and visit some 15 county jails each year, preaching the salvation of Jesus Christ and the power of the Holy Spirit."

I didn't say anything more to give him time to write down what I'd just said. After about a minute, he looked up at me.

"Got it down. The next board is *Thy will be done*. So I guess I pray to follow God's will, right? You know, ask that God's will be done in me. His will isn't for me to keep drinking and using. So when I pray His will be done, it's like praying He'll show me how to stop drinking and taking drugs.

"And reading the Bible every day would be His will, and praying continually, and other stuff like that, right?"

"That's right on the mark, Scott. Here's a Scripture verse about God's will you should meditate on."

Do not conform to the pattern of this world, but be transformed by the renewing of your mind. Then you will be able to test and approve what God's will is – his good, pleasing and perfect will.

Romans 12:2

"The pattern of this fallen world is dark and dangerous, and you don't want to follow its ways. Instead you want to be aligned with the Kingdom of God and learn what His will is."

"Got it, Pat, but how do I renew my mind?"

"You don't. The Holy Spirit renews your mind when you read His Word in the Bible and seek God with all your heart."

"Question, Pat. How do I seek God with all my heart?"

"We covered reading the Bible last week and are covering prayer today. Next week we'll explore other ways."

Scott wrote that all down in his notebook. I couldn't get over how good of a note taker he was. I'm always a bit wary when having a discussion like this with someone who doesn't write anything down. How are they going to remember it all?

"I'll bet there's more to it than that, right, Pat?"

"You're correct again. That's what's so great about using the Lord's prayer as a guide to more in-depth prayer. There's always more to it than that.

"For example, you can pray God's will to be done with your family, friends, co-workers, and people you meet every day."

Scott wrote that down but didn't lift his head for what came next. I guessed he was pondering what he'd just written down.

"I don't know quite how to say this, Pat, but how do we know what God's will is for someone else? I mean, how do I know that praying for my brother to get the job he's applied for is God's will? Or that my son becomes the quarterback of his little league team because that's what he wants?"

"The simple answer is 'you don't.' In the second chapter of John, at the wedding in Cana, Mary, Jesus' mother, simply tells Him, *They have no more wine*. She didn't tell Him what she thought He should do. She left it in His hands.

"You don't have to offer God a strategy for your brother. You can simple pray something like this, 'Lord, my brother needs a new job, but he needs something more important. He needs your saving grace to be born again. If this is the job where that might somehow happen, I pray You show him favor. If another job would be better for that, I pray for that job to roll in.'

"And for your son, 'Lord, protect the health of my son wherever he ends up. Build a hedge of protection around him both in his physical pursuits and in his spiritual development. If being quarterback would be the best thing for him, I pray You help pave the way. If another position might fit the talents you gave him better, help him see what your will is for him.' Does this make sense to you, Scott?"

"Wow! Wow! Absolutely! That's a whole new way of praying. I shouldn't be praying for my will to be done, I mean, like I know what's best for my brother or my son. God knows what's best, and that's what I should be praying for."

It was time to move on to the next board.

"The first four boards have to do with God; the last three with us. I shaded them to show the division.

"What're your thoughts on *Give us this day our daily bread?*"

"Well, given that things have been going in two's lately, I'd say it means God providing me food, a job, and all the other stuff I need to live."

I nodded.

"And it probably means what's in the booklet my wife reads every morning – *Our Daily Bread*. And I guess it probably means something else, right?"

"You've done pretty well on this one, Scott. But remember, you're not a lone wolf in this world. This is the place in the Lord's Prayer where you pray for others – for Aunt Mable's arthritis, your friend Jack's addiction, all the members of your family, Mary's breakup with her husband…"

"You mean in the way we pray about God's will right? I used to pray that God would heal Aunt Mable's arthritis, but that's my will, right? Help me out on this one, Pat."

"I would use a *lifting-up* prayer for Aunt Mable, something like this, 'Father, my aunt is in great discomfort with arthritis. I lift her up to Your mercy and compassion. Show her Your presence in her suffering and let her know that You will never leave her or forsake her. And if You would cure her arthritis, what a fantastic testimony that would be to You! In Jesus' name, amen.'"

The look on Scott's face was somewhere between relief and thankfulness, like someone had invited him to step out of a barren landscape into a warm and welcoming home.

"You've given me a whole new look at prayer, Pat. I'm starting to see how I can pray continually without being bored out of my mind or saying the same stuff over and over."

We talked several more minutes about our daily bread and how God provides us with all we need, both physical and spiritual, especially the spiritual. Scott kept his pen moving.

"Scott, we've covered this petition pretty well. Let's take a look at *Forgive us our trespasses as we forgive those who trespass against us.*

"This doesn't mean we keep confessing the same sins over and over. We confess what we've done or not done of late. For me, it's losing my temper with my wife or not reading the Bible for two days. For you, it might be having 'just one little drink' at the bar with your friends. Or sleeping late on a Sunday morning instead of going to church with your wife and kids.

"But it's more than just saying you're sorry for doing or not doing something. It's repenting of what you've done, which means promising not to do it again. Remorse is one thing; repentance is something else entirely."

"Absolutely, I've already repented of not going to church. I've told Liz I'd be going with her and the kids from now on. It's like I've drawn a line in the sand to never miss church on Sunday. But what if I don't go one Sunday? What happens with my repentance and my promise and the line in the sand?"

"Simple. We're not perfect people. If you miss a Sunday, repent of it, beg your wife for forgiveness, and draw another line in the sand. Just don't be doing that too often, or you'll lose her trust and respect.

"You can do the same thing with having a wee small drink. Don't beat yourself up or let Satan accuse you of being a loser. Repent and draw another line in the sand that you'll never drink again. And acknowledge to God that you don't want to lose His presence or your family. Remember it's a process. If you do cross a line, hopefully you don't draw a new line and cross it the next day. The distance between lines should be getting greater and greater until you no longer cross them.

"I think the forgiving others is self-explanatory, right?"

Scott nodded.

We were at the last board – *And lead us not into temptation but deliver us from the evil one.*

"I get the deliver us from Satan, but why would God lead us into temptation?"

"My take is that we're asking God to lead us in paths away from temptation. For you, Scott, that would mean asking God to lead you away from your suppliers of meth and the friends you used with and the stress that puts you in temptation's way."

"I got it now, Pat. I didn't before. Now I know how to pray continually; but knowing you, I'll bet there's other stuff."

"There's always other stuff, Scott, but you need to walk before you run. Let's talk about prayer in general, and then I'll give you one more technique for prayer and we'll end there."

"I'm on board," Scott said with a laugh.

"Probably the most important thing about prayer is to see it from God's standpoint. We need to pass from thinking about God as part of our life to realizing we're part of His life. When we make that change in viewpoint, God mysteriously moves from the edges of our prayer experience to the very center."

I watched as Scott wrote that down in his notebook and then drew a circle around it, and then put two asterisks in front of the circle. When he saw I was watching him, he smiled.

I looked at the clock on the wall. He looked at me looking and saw we had ten minutes left.

"Pat, are you going to be able to give that one more technique before we have to leave?"

"No problem. It's easy to understand, Scott. We'll get through it guaranteed, unless you ask too many questions."

"My mouth is shut and my ears are open."

"I call it *praying at every turn*, which means you pray every time you change from doing one thing to something else. For example, when you get up in the morning, you pray. And when you go into the bathroom to get ready for the day, and when you make coffee and eat breakfast. Then you pray on the way to work and over the emails you read first thing and before every interaction with a different person. And you keep going like that until you go to bed at night. Does that make sense?"

"It does, but what do I pray about?"

"Don't worry about that. The Holy Spirit will show you. You've prayed little because of your self-dependence. When you see that your life depends on God, you'll pray much."

We scheduled to meet again in one week. He came through on reading the Bible faithfully each day, but with what we covered on prayer, would he be able to incorporate all of that into his life, or would he give up halfway through the week? I planned to pray for Scott much during the next seven days.

Chapter Ten
Step 6: The rest of the plan.

And I, when I am lifted up from the earth, will draw all people to myself.

John 12:32

Jesus is like a magnet. The closer we come to Him, the more powerful is His force to draw us to Himself.

We receive the Holy Spirit at the point of our salvation. We're always in His presence because His presence is always in our spirits. When we, by poor choices, move away from Him in our souls, His drawing power becomes weaker and weaker, and we're wide open to go our own way and the way of the world.

How do we draw near to Him? We've already found that reading the Bible daily and praying continually are two very important ways. In this chapter, we'll uncover six more.

SCOTT'S STORY PART 3

The next week arrived as certainly as the next hour, and we were back in the coffee shop conference room.

We had picked up our usual coffee pot and two mugs at the counter and were filling them when I asked Scott the question that was at the front of my mind.

"Well, Scott, how did the last week go with your praying?"

"Unbelievable," he answered before taking a slow sip of very hot coffee. "I thanked God at every turn the first day, thinking about how you said to pray like your life depends on Him. I started praying the

Our Father like you showed me in the early morning and throughout the day and before I went to sleep at night. That went *really* well.

"The morning of the third day, I remembered about how the Holy Spirit would show me what to say when I pray at every turn. I thought I'd done pretty good on my own, but now I wanted to know what the Holy Spirit had to say.

"'Show me the way, Holy Spirit,' I said, and He did. Out of the blue came this idea to pray verses from Scripture."

I'd used that method for years but hadn't wanted to bring it up to Scott and overwhelm him. How exciting that the Holy Spirit introduced him to use that method of prayer!

"How do you select the verses?"

"That's the funny part. I don't; the Holy Spirit does. You know, I was reading the 5th chapter of Matthew Saturday morning when I bumped into The Beatitudes. I'd never heard about them before. Then a voice within me instructed me to pray the eight beatitudes, one each day. Today is *Blessed are the merciful, for they will be shown mercy.* I guess when I've gotten through all of them, He'll show me what verses come next."

Was this the same Scott I first met with three weeks ago? He couldn't have learned to become a man of prayer so quickly on his own. The power of the Holy Spirit renewed his thinking and habits. He was no longer a natural man following his own will; He was a spiritual man transformed by the Holy Spirit.

"Do you pray for everyone you meet each day and for every meeting or encounter you have?" I asked, with a view to moving on to the next three ways to stay near God.

"Absolutely, I could tell you a lot more, but I'm hoping to find out what else I can do to stick to Jesus like glue."

He was on the same track I was. I poured more coffee into my mug and walked over to the whiteboard.

"We spent lots of time on the first two pieces of the plan because they're so critical. The others are important as well but easier to understand. What do you think's next?"

He sat back and rolled the question over in his mind.

"Well, church has to fit in there someplace, I guess."

I wrote *Attend a Spirit-filled church* on the board and put a 3 in front of it.

"Let's take a look at *Church*." I asked Scott to turn to Hebrews 10:24-25 and read it out loud:

> *And let us consider how we may spur one another on toward*
> *love and good deeds, not giving up meeting together, as some*
> *are in the habit of doing, but encouraging one another.*

"Very good, Scott. The early church emphasized meeting together. Their gatherings were Spirit-filled and consisted of praise, worship, songs, and learning about Jesus Christ. However, not all churches today are Spirit-filled. Some preach more of a social gospel. There's nothing wrong about that, but you need a church that'll teach you about the real Jesus and has mostly members who are serious Christ-followers."

"That's the kind of church my wife goes to, and I sometimes go with her. But I'd better go all the time, huh?"

"Yes, as in every Sunday unless you absolutely can't. And you want to do more than just go to church. You want to be involved in it – like join a Bible study, be an usher, show up for cleaning days, and be part of other church activities."

Scott wrote all that down.

"That brings us to the fourth item, Scott," as I wrote down *Hang around fellow believers* and put a 4 in front of it. "I'm not going to tell you who *not* to hang around with. I'm going to tell you who *to* hang around with, and that's fellow believers. You'll find them when you help out in your church. You'll also find them with *Be involved in Bible studies*, which I wrote on the board and put a 5 in front of it."

Scott had a bit of a smirk on his face.

"Where's that in the Bible, Pat? You said this was the Bible's plan, not yours or my plan. You probably have the passage right at your fingertips."

I smiled because I did have the verse right at my fingertips. I turned to Matthew 18:20 and read:

> *For where two or three gather in my name, there am I with them.*

"Well, you knocked those two off fast," Scott said as he wrote them down. "How many are left?"

"How many do you think are left, Scott?"

"Probably about a hundred, but there's not time for that. How about two more biggies. That'll bring us to seven and that'll be manageable and that'll finish us off for time anyway."

Scott was on the low end with 100 ways to stay near Jesus, but we *didn't* have time to cover such things as reading devotionals and Christian books, playing Christian music on the radio, or attending Christian conferences and retreats. Plus, even a list of fifteen would've flooded his mind and capsized his memory.

"Two it will be, then. There's a very important one that I don't want to miss. Do you want to make a guess?"

He shook his head no.

"I need to stay close to Jesus as much as you do, Scott. This next one is why I'm meeting with you and why I'm a chaplain at the Wright County Jail and why I visit jails and rehab facilities throughout Minnesota. Take a look at James 1:1 and that should inform you what the sixth item is."

Scott flipped to James 1:1 and read:

James, a servant of God and of the Lord Jesus Christ.

"Now turn to Mark 10:45 and read that one and then tell me what the sixth item is:

For even the Son of Man did not come to be served, but to serve, and to give his life as a ransom for many.

"*Service in Christ's name,*" Scott said with a look of certainty.

"Exactly. Do you need any more explanation than that?"

I didn't think he would. Scott looked at the clock.

"We only have thirty minutes left. I'll let the Holy Spirit reveal the rest of it to me in the morning."

How marvelous! That was a major insight. He didn't have to figure out everything. He had a Helper to inform him.

"What's the last one?"

I wrote it on the board and put a number 7 before it; *Tell others about Jesus.*

"That means to tell your family and friends that you have decided to follow Jesus and let Him lead you to sobriety and take over your life."

Scott raised his hand to signal he wanted to interrupt me. He was breathing fast.

"That's what I wanted to tell you right away. I didn't tell my wife I was going to stop drinking and taking drugs, like you told me not to do. She'd heard that promise a hundred times before. I told her about our meeting together and that I'd decided to follow Jesus, no turning back. She gave me a hug that I think cracked a few ribs. And she told me that's what she'd been praying for the last five years. Then she cried. So did I."

I was close to tears myself for the transformation of one man following Jesus and a marriage saved.

"That's fantastic, Scott. Your wife is already a believer. Have you talked to anyone else in your family or any friends that aren't believers or are weak Christians?"

"No. I'm afraid to. Who am I to tell anyone how to live their lives? Why would anyone who knows me listen to a word I say?"

"You don't have to tell them what they should or shouldn't do or teach them about Jesus. You only have to tell them your story. It's called sharing your testimony. That's what Jesus told the man He'd just freed from a legion of demons in Mark 5:19:"

> *Go home to your own people and tell them how much the*
> *Lord has done for you, and how he has had mercy on you.*

The clock turned to 10 a.m., and we were done. Before we went out own ways, I prayed for Scott and encouraged him to make the plan he'd learned from the Bible a daily habit.

I also told him in no uncertain terms that he couldn't walk this journey on his own. He needed some strong Christians to walk alongside him and help him stay in the light, because the world and its temptations would always be nearby waiting to reel him in like a floundering fish.

"Well, Pat, I have a live-in Christian I can lean on – my wife. And I have a close friend who led me to Christ ten years ago and's been bugging me ever since to become more Christ-like, as he puts it. He'd be overjoyed to walk alongside me, as you say. Is that what you mean?"

I smiled when I said, "It's exactly what I mean."

As we left the room, this is what remained on the whiteboard, with the 8th item just added:

1. Read the Bible daily.
2. Pray continually.
3. Attend a Spirit-filled church.
4. Hang around fellow believers.
5. Be involved in Bible studies.
6. Service in Christ's name.
7. Tell others about Jesus.
8. Have at least one strong Christian to serve as a mentor.

Chapter Eleven
Step 7: Execute the plan.

"All this," David said, "I have in writing as a result of the Lord's hand on me, and he enabled me to understand all the details of the plan."

1 Chronicles 28:19

A certain man walked into a gas station and asked for directions to a certain church that had promised to help him get back on his feet. He was penniless, homeless, and hadn't had a job for two months.

He listened carefully to the directions given him, since he hadn't been in that part of town before. When the station manager asked if he understood how to get to the church, he answered, "Perfectly!"

Then he stepped out the door and walked to the end of the first block, returned back to the station, and sat down on a couch against the far wall. At the end of the day, he left the station and went back home.

This story demonstrates how those with a plan to change their lives may execute it poorly or not at all.

BRYAN'S STORY

During a Gideon's Sunday afternoon Bible study at the Wright County Jail, Bryan made a heartfelt decision to accept Jesus Christ as his Savior and follow Him and live in His light.

He attended church services every Sunday in jail and hung around other Christian believers in his unit who encouraged him in his new-found faith. He started reading the Bible for at least two hours a day. He became part of a prayer group in the jail and learned how to be a prayer warrior.

Bryan talked to other inmates about how he'd lived in darkness until he came into the light of Christ. He then encouraged them to make the same decision. In short, he was an on-fire Christian and an ambassador for Christ.

A few days before he was released, Bryan and I talked about what he'd do to stop using and stay out of jail. With determination in his voice and a face of flint, he opened the conversation with a proclamation I've heard many times.

"I'm serious, Chaplain. This is my last time in jail. When I'm outta here, I'm outta here for good."

No doubt he believed that vow. I was less certain.

"Are you sure about that, Bryan, that you'll never set foot in jail again? I hope that's true for you, but what's your plan?"

He looked at me as if I'd asked him for the blueprint of the jail we were in at that moment.

"I just told you my plan. I'm done with jail and never coming back. Done deal. Never going to set foot in here again."

"That's not much of a plan, Bryan. How about all the things we talked about?"

"I thought we called that a roadmap, you know, reading the Bible and praying and the other stuff I wrote down. Is that watcha mean by a plan?"

He was referring to the find-it-in-the-Bible routine I did with Scott in the last three chapters.

"Well, a roadmap describes the *what* and *why*. A plan to execute describes the *how*."

"Whatever. But I just told you I'm not coming back. That's my plan. I wasn't a Christian when I was selling and using drugs before. Now I am. That'll keep me out of jail, that and the stuff I got written down from our talking, you know, the roadmap."

Bryan sounded like the man who walked into the gas station. He knew the directions (the roadmap) but wasn't committed to following them. He was sincere but naïve, like a brave young soldier going into his first battle, not realizing the enemy was as well-equipped as he was.

I needed to challenge him, but wanted to do so nicely. I asked in as casual a voice as I could muster.

"Do you plan to read the Bible every day like in here?"

"Of course, maybe more like an hour a day cause of getting a job and a place to stay and stuff like that. But I'll read it every day, sure I will.

"And I'll be praying every day like we all talked about and finding a Spirit-filled church to go to and getting into a Bible study right away. You know, and the other stuff you talked to me about. I got it all written down. If that's what you mean by a plan, I got it.

"And I'm gonna go to Celebrate Recovery and Narcotics Anonymous meetings on a regular basis like we talked about. That's in my roadmap too, I mean my plan. I know I need to do that. Like you said, I can't do it on my own."

I sighed and decided not to push any harder. I'd only antagonize him. He didn't understand the difference between a plan as something written down on a piece of paper (a roadmap) and a plan to execute (that is, carry out) what's written down.

"That's great, Bryan. Make sure to call me once a week, so I can keep up with how you're doing."

"I sure will, Pat. I sure will."

I didn't doubt his sincerity. He was a man with a roadmap, but I'd seen inmates with roadmaps before and they ended up back in jail because they didn't execute them successfully. I hoped Bryan wouldn't be one of them.

I received my first call from him exactly one week later.

"I've got my plan right in front of me, Pat, and it's keeping me straight. I've got a job interview tomorrow at a fabrication plant. They need ten welders for a big contract."

"Sounds great, Bryan. Text me if you get the job, and then we'll talk again in a week."

"Sure thing, Pat."

I could tell he was excited by the animated way he talked, like a little kid telling a friend that his parents had bought him his first bike.

I received a text the next day in the early evening. *Got job. Started today. Much work. $19 hour. Lots overtime. 12 hours today. Work Sat.* 😎 *$$$*

I texted back. *Great news but concerned with all the hours. How are you able to follow the plan?*

He texted me back the next day. *No time for plan right now. Working too many hours. No time for trouble. Get home, go bed. Have time in 3 weeks – big contract done.*

I called Bryan the following Sunday at noon. I was starting to become concerned about a relapse. He answered on the sixth ring and sounded like he'd just woken up.

"How are you doing, Bryan?"

I could barely hear him mumble and stumble.

"Not so good. They sold the house I'm staying in and I gotta find somewhere else. And I just found out my mother has cancer and won't live but a couple months. It's comen down on me hard, Pat. I was at a friend's place, and he was smokin meth. I almost had some, but I made a promise I ain't gonna break."

I didn't hear from Bryan after that. He didn't answer my calls or texts. Four weeks later he showed up in jail. He'd been drinking in a bar and got into a fight. His probation officer wrote him up and back to jail he came, the same jail he vowed never to set foot in again.

I saw him in the programs area, with his head down, trying to pretend he didn't see me.

"Bryan," I said in a voice he couldn't ignore, "Let's talk."

The programs sergeant gave a thumbs up, and off we went to a meeting room. Bryan decided to get in the first word when I shut the door.

"What can I say, Pat? I screwed up royally. My life was a mess. I couldn't find a place to stay and moved in with my meth-using friend. I was working longer and longer hours. My father didn't want me to come home to see my mother. He told me she doesn't need a drug addict and felon around. My girlfriend told me to get lost. I couldn't take it any longer and took some meth to handle life. But it was always at my friend's place so I didn't get picked up. Then I started drinking, went to a bar, got into a fight, and here I am."

"What about the plan you walked out of here with?"

I'm not surprised he didn't answer me. He didn't say anything, and I didn't say anything.

With his head down and his voice faltering, he broke the silence.

"I didn't have time to do much about the plan. I went to church the first Sunday and made one Celebrate Recovery meeting and showed up for NA once. I found a guy there who said he'd be my sponsor, but I never got back to him."

He started to tear up.

"I guess I know what you mean by a plan now. I had a list of stuff to do. You called it my roadmap. But I couldn't do it, Pat. I said I could but I couldn't cause I didn't have a plan to pull it off. I read the Bible maybe a couple times and only prayed before meals, and then not even that. Life gobbled me up. I lost Jesus big time."

It's hard to see a grown man cry out of hopelessness. I spoke in a soft voice.

"You're right when you say you can't do it on your own. None of us can."

He looked up, and the tears poured out.

"What can I do then, Pat? How can I ever stay sober and out of jail? I'm bout ready to just give up."

He acted surprised and stopped crying when I said, "That's a great place to be, Bryan."

"What?" he said with a look of disbelief. "How can it be a good thing to give up?"

"Because when you come to the end of yourself, then God can take over. Do you want to let him take over the life you've given up on?"

Bryan was at a loss for words and could only sputter out an, "I guess. What other choice do I have?"

"Do you have the roadmap you left here with?" I asked.

"You mean the one I didn't have a plan to follow?" he said with a fake laugh.

"Yes, the plan you didn't do anything about. It's like the blueprint of a house, Scott. It doesn't do anyone any good unless workers come to a site with materials and a plan to build the house from the blueprint.

I didn't smile. I didn't frown. I spoke matter-of-factly. It was time to get down to business.

Bryan had a face that reflected mine.

"I still have the plan in my Bible."

I smiled to put Bryan at ease and spoke with an encouraging voice.

"I'll be here next week on Thursday. Bring your Bible and the written plan with you, and we'll talk about how you can execute that plan in real life and real time."

Next Thursday arrived, and Bryan and I were in the same meeting room.

"Here's the plan," Bryan said.

I leaned forward in my chair.

"What value does this have, Bryan?"

He seemed to know where I was going.

"No value if I don't carry it out. Can you tell me how to come up with a plan to do that?"

His voice was too lukewarm. He needed to be on fire if this was going to work.

"Do what, Bryan?"

He gave me a funny look.

"Show me how to carry out God's plan for my life! What did you think I meant?"

This time his voice had some passion in it.

"Is that what you really want, Bryan, more than anything else in this world?"

I think he understood what I was looking for as he stared me in the eyes.

"Yes, Pat, that's what I really want. If you want me to write out in my own blood that I'm committed to following through with God's plan for my life, I'll do it. A gallon of my blood if that's needed."

I laughed.

"I don't think a gallon of your blood is needed, Bryan. Maybe a half-pint will do."

He laughed.

"OK, a half-pint then."

I got up, opened the door, and walked down to the Programs office where I picked up five sheets of typing paper and a borrowed pen that I promised to bring back. Sgt. Francine lifted her eyebrows.

"We have a little writing assignment for Bryan?" she asked.

"Indeed we do," I chuckled.

When I returned to the meeting room, I handed the paper and pen to Bryan before I sat down.

"Get ready to start writing, Bryan. You're going to write down how you'll execute God's plan – step by step."

He grabbed one sheet of paper, put it on the table diagonally in a writing position, and put the pen at the top.

"I guess what we're going to do is come up with a plan to execute the plan."

"You have it."

I pushed my chair back and walked over to the whiteboard fixed to the wall.

"Let's start with a plan to read the Bible daily. Before we do that, do you understand now that you can't take a job or get so involved in other things to the point where you don't have time to carry out your roadmap of freedom from drugs and jail?"

His head dropped down in shame.

"I've got that. I won't make that mistake again. I'd put two gallons of blood up against that."

With that, he laughed. I was glad to see him both deadly serious and joking around.

I wrote on the board *Read the Bible Daily* and put a 1 in front of it.

"You can't just *say* you're going to read the Bible every day. You've got to have a strategy to *execute* it. I'd suggest you set up a half-hour in the morning to read the Bible, meditate on it, and pray about what you're reading. Then do that again before you go to sleep at night – so it's the first thing you do in the morning and the last thing you do at night. I'd also suggest you keep the small Gideon Bible I gave you in your pocket for during the day. And you do all that without fail."

Bryan was writing furiously on the paper I'd given him.

"How about prayer, Bryan?"

Bryan finished writing about reading the Bible and looked up.

"About the same as the Bible. I didn't have time."

I sighed, not because I didn't expect this to happen but because what I feared would happen happened.

"You remember how we talked about the Lord's prayer being the outline of all prayer, right?"

He nodded like a little boy who'd just admitted to his mother that he'd forgotten to bring his schoolwork home.

"You can pray the Lord's Prayer throughout the day, one petition at a time. For example, you can acknowledge the glory of God and bless His name during your morning Bible reading time. And you can pray that He shows you how to advance His kingdom that day. At any point during the day, when you have choices to make, you can pray, 'Not my will but Thine be done.' Set a goal that you'll ask His will be done at least five times during any day."

I paused to let Bryan catch up with his writing.

"I think I got it," he said. "I can also thank God at least five times a day for giving me what I need to live – my daily bread. I think I'll ask Him to lead me away from temptation situations in my morning time with Him and again during the day if I get a call from my meth-using buddy to come over that night to chill out."

I felt a good vibration in my bones that he was getting it.

"How about the forgiving and being forgiven?"

Bryan's eyes twinkled.

"I was getting to that, Pat. I'd do that before going to sleep as a final look at the day. I'll ask God's forgiveness for the things I did or didn't do that didn't follow His commandments. Like, He tells me to love others, but maybe I said a harsh word at the grocery store when I had to wait too long in line. And I could forgive the checker for talking to the customer in front of me who was obviously someone she knew. You know, stuff like that."

I smiled and challenged Bryan.

"What about the things you didn't do that day that you should have?"

"I was about to get to that. If I didn't read the Bible as planned or fell short on praying throughout the day or thanking God at least five times, I'd repent about that before going to sleep and promise to do better the next day. With the power of the Holy Spirit I might add. I know I can't keep up on my own. I've proven that too many times."

I sat there with my mouth parted and my eyebrows arched. He knew more than I gave him credit for.

"Great. You have a built-in checklist to review the day. What else is on that list?"

"If it's a Sunday, did I go to church not only in body but also in spirit? If it's a Tuesday, did I go to the Celebrate Recovery meeting at 7 p.m.? If it's an every other Wednesday, did I attend my Narcotics Anonymous meeting?"

I sat back in my chair and let Bryan continue. I told myself I wouldn't interrupt him again until he was done describing his check-list at the end of each day.

He continued on.

"I think I'll set a goal of having at least three Christian friends that I can talk to about Jesus. That one'll be easy. I already have you I'll be talking to once a week. And my drug addiction sponsor is a believer I'll touch base with once a week. That only leaves one believer a week to talk to."

I'd promised myself not to interrupt him with additional questions, but I felt I needed to offer him some advice here.

"That's really good Bryan. Three is enough for now. You need to be careful not to set the bar too high that you can't reach it. Then you'll kick yourself for not living up to your goals. You can always reset your number of Christian people you hang around with later. Okay, I'll keep my mouth shut now and let you go on."

"No, no, Pat. I need advice. Like you said, I can't do it on my own."

He wrote down what I'd said with an asterisk in front of it.

"I think I've got two left – joining a Bible study and Christian service, right?"

"Right."

"The Bible study should be easy for me. I'm gonna give myself three weeks to find one that works best. Then it'll be like Celebrate Recovery and NA. I go whenever it meets, unless I absolutely can't, other than that I'm tired or too busy or something like that. A Saturday morning group might be a good bet for me."

I wanted to encourage him to set his own plan, so I supported what he said.

"Yes, a Saturday morning would be a good time, and I think you won't have any trouble finding a group that meets then."

"Got it," he said as he wrote it down. "But I'm going to need your help on Christian service."

Bryan had a Bible in front of him, and I told him to read James 1:1.

James, a servant of God and of the Lord Jesus Christ.

"What does that tell you, Bryan?"

"That I gotta be a Christian servant, but how can I do that, you know, like more than once or twice a week?"

"Here's one idea for you, Bryan. Keep a five-dollar bill in your billfold in a separate place and call it God's pocket. Then when you see someone begging at a roadside or someone in need in a grocery store, you give him or her the five dollars. That way you'll be looking to do God's work wherever you go. Ask the Holy Spirit who to give it to, and let Him show you."

"Got it. How often do I do that? I don't have a lot of money."

"At least once a month, more when you can afford it. And when your church asks you to help clean on a Saturday, that's Christian service, plus you'll be around fellow believers. If a car wants to merge ahead of you on a busy road, let it. If a woman asks if she can go ahead of you in a grocery line, let her."

"OK, Pat, I think I got it. And that's something I can think about at the end of the day – did I perform any Christian service today. And If I didn't, I confess it and make sure to do something in Christ's name the next day."

I told Bryan he had an impressive plan to execute his original plan and an excellent way to do a check on himself at the end of each day. We could go over his list when we talked each week and review his progress in becoming a mature Christian.

Bryan exited the jail three months later.

At first he called me every week without fail. Then we agreed to every two weeks. And now we touch base once a month. We have stayed in touch for the past four years, and Bryan is one of the strongest Christians I know. He understands he can't go it alone. He needs Jesus and other believers to help him.

Bryan now sponsors another man trying to bury a drug addiction, and Bryan has a girlfriend who's a strong believer and is a helpmate for him in staying on the right path. I think they'll be married soon.

Not everyone I work with is a Bryan. He'd grown up in a family who went to church every Sunday. His parents insisted that he attend Sunday School and a Wednesday evening youth group at church. He knew what it meant to study the Bible and pray. His parents demonstrated with their lives what it meant to serve others in Christ's name. In short, he had the background to understand the pieces of the plan I showed him.

But Bryan only nibbled around the corners of religion. He didn't dive into it like his parents or his two sisters. He'd never invited Jesus into his heart; and when he graduated from high school, he went his own way and the way of the world. He had been exposed to the light, but he had chosen the darkness instead.

How about addicts and inmates and others in dark places who haven't had an introduction to the light of the Kingdom of God like Bryan? How about brand new Christians who need to start out simple? The next chapter is as simple as it gets.

Chapter Twelve
I have decided to follow Jesus.

Remain in Me, and I [will remain] in you. Just as no branch can bear fruit by itself without remaining in the vine, neither can you [bear fruit, producing evidence of your faith] unless you remain in Me.

John 15:4 AMP

This is what a personal relationship to Jesus Christ looks like, in His own words. It's like a blood transfusion. You're old, tired diseased blood is replaced by His life-giving blood that makes you alive in Christ, the light of the world.

There's only one simple thing you need to do to change your darkness into light as a steady diet.

A HIJACKED CHAPEL MESSAGE

A strong wind rocked my car on June 12, 2017, as I drove the 35 miles from my house to the Minneapolis Adult and Teen Challenge. In an hour and a half, I'd be giving 8 a.m. chapel to some 300 men and women, the first time I'd done such a thing.

With so many people and my first time giving chapel anywhere, I wrote out more notes than I usually did. I had a two-page outline with some pieces found in this book. I'd rehearsed the outline five times and felt comfortably in my comfort zone.

As I zipped through the last traffic light in Buffalo and entered the open highway, the Holy Spirit caught my attention. I'm not a *Thus sayeth the Lord* kind of guy. That means I don't hear God speaking directly to me in a voice that comes out of a burning bush or a dove hovering over my car. And I don't hear the voice of God in a word-for-word manner with my inner ears. Once I did some 40-some years ago when He spoke directly to me with words that changed the course of my life at a time of great anguish and confusion. And one other time, but that's it.

When the Holy Spirit wants to catch my attention, He does so with thoughts and ideas and pictures that I put into my own words. If someone else were given the same thought, they might express it quite differently. Or He'll speak to me through people and circumstances that are often unexpected. In this case, the thought that jumped into my mind was far-out and scary.

It arrived more as a picture than words, just as a 40 mph wind pushed my car toward a ditch. *Throw your notes into the back of the car. I'll give you what to say.*

I pulled the car back into the driving lane and cried out.

"Speak to 300 people without a note? That's crazy."

But the thought wouldn't go away. The Holy Spirit has a persistence that can be both annoying and freeing, depending on one's frame of mind. He wouldn't let it go. What could I do?

"Okay, fine then. I'll do it," I said, as I tossed the notes into the back seat, like an old newspaper thrown into a garbage can.

"Are you satisfied now, Lord? I'm going to make a fool of myself when I stumble in front of all those people, but if that's what you want, then I'll do it." I wasn't a happy camper.

I sensed a smile on God's face as the following verse popped into my mind:

> *Do not worry beforehand about what to say. Just say*
> *whatever is given you at the time, for it is not you speaking,*
> *but the Holy Spirit.*

Mark 13:11

I begged the Holy Spirit to at least give me a clue of what to say at chapel. He didn't hesitate. I already had a power-point slide of a radio dial, and He directed me to use that as an illustration. The other thing that crept into my mind was the song, *I Have Decided to Follow Jesus*, which I knew by heart.

"Anything else, Lord?"

There was nothing more.

"So that's it? What happened to a three-point sermon?"

I could almost hear a laugh and a nod of the head. I prayed the rest of the way in thanksgiving that the Holy Spirit was in charge and wouldn't let me die on the stage.

When I arrived at the Minneapolis Adult and Teen Challenge, I headed straight to the sound booth and asked if they could play *I Have Decided to Follow Jesus* as the last song of the customary three-song set.

"No problem," said the soundman.

As the three songs played, the worship taking place in the auditorium nearly blew me away. Arms were raised, men and women went to the front to bow down and pray, hugs were given and received, jubilation ran rampant. I practically floated up on the stage when it came my turn for a 40-minute message.

I felt the Holy Spirit coursing through my veins as I spoke what He wanted me to say. When I told them a story about someone being saved, they cheered and clapped their hands. One woman gave a loud whistle. They were on fire for Jesus. They were more than listeners; they were lively participants.

I never knew exactly what was coming next as I spoke. It was freeing to let the Holy Spirit be in charge, and it's now the way I give most presentations.

I skipped most of the slides I'd prepared on Power Point and moved to the radio station illustration:

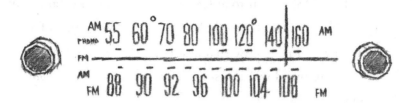

In turn, their attention was riveted on the slide of the radio dial illustration. I could hear some comments, "What's this all about?" and, "What's a radio dial got to do with Jesus?" I paused for a few seconds to let them ponder the drawing before talking.

"Think of your inner life as a radio station dial. The Holy Spirit station is 160 on the dial, where you hear God loud and clear. On the other end at 55 is the station of the world, Satan, and your own self-seeking self, where you can barely hear God.

"The closer you are to 160, the safer you are. The closer to 55, the more danger you face. If you do nothing to stay near 160, you slowly but surely drift back toward 55. You promise yourself it'll be different this time when you finish your stay here. You'll stay tuned to Jesus. But you've made that promise before and you've broken that promise before – some of you five times or fifteen times or more.

"Coming to Adult and Teen Challenge greatly increases your chances to keep your promise this time. A few addicts can stay sober long-term through their own will power. Most can't. I've found that those likelihoods are reversed for those who go through the 13-month Adult and Teen Challenge program – most of you will stay sober and only a few will start using again. I pray my message will help you in the ongoing struggle.

"Here's the hard facts: when you leave here, you go back to the same places and the same people and the same stresses in your life. It's hard getting a job when you're known as an alcoholic or drug addict or both. Some of you are felons. Some members of your family don't want to have anything to do with you. Maybe you have a restraining order against you? It's tough.

"You no longer have the time to stay tuned to the Holy Spirit station, and you drift to the station where the ways of the world, your own wants, and the temptations of Satan play so loudly that you lose touch with the Jesus you heard so clearly here. Your focus becomes your problems and the necessities of life that need taking care of – food, shelter, clothing, a job, family, friends, and all the other distractions that are a part of life. In other words, life gets in the way, and there's more of you and the world in your life than there is of Jesus. You see, that's the answer to the question of how you go back to alcohol and drugs over and over again.

"Without being tuned to the Holy Spirit station, you're left with your own strength, and that's not enough to resist temptations. In a moment of weakness or when a serious problem comes up, you'll take one drink or use meth and throw your sobriety out the window.

"Now, what are you going to do to keep yourself so tuned to God that you'll never use again? I'm not talking concepts anymore. Concepts won't do you any good unless you act on them. I'm going to explain what you can do to stay close to the Holy Spirit Station."

Echoes of *Amen* and *Lay it on us, brother* reverberated throughout the auditorium.

I'll not recount here all that I told them, but pieces of what you've read in the last four chapters came to me. It was time to end chapel with the song the Holy Spirit directed me to discuss.

"The last song played this morning was *I Have Decided to Follow Jesus.* Let me tell you the story behind that song. In the 1800s, a missionary came to Northeast India to a tribe of very violent people. Nokseng, his wife, and two boys accepted Jesus as their Savior.

"The chief demanded they renounce Jesus. Nokseng answered, 'No, I have decided to follow Jesus. No turning back.' The chief had the two boys killed. Nokseng then announced, 'Though none go with me, I still will follow.' The chief had his wife killed.

"Before Nokseng was killed, he prayed, 'The cross before me, the world behind me, I have decided to follow Jesus.' And the testimony of that village is that this display of faith led to the conversion of the chief and the whole village."

You could've heard a pin drop in that auditorium filled with 300 boisterous men and women who were unashamed to demonstrate their feelings about Jesus.

"You know, brothers and sisters, we've talked about many things today, but let me make it as simple as I can. If you're willing to follow Jesus in the midst of all your troubles and woes, you'll get along just fine."

At that I sang the song from memory. When I finished, everyone stood up and clapped for the Holy Spirit. It certainly wasn't for me, since I'm not the one who orchestrated the talk nor can I sing very well:

I have decided to follow Jesus;
I have decided to follow Jesus;
I have decided to follow Jesus;
No turning back, no turning back.

The world behind me, the cross before me;
The world behind me, the cross before me;
The world behind me, the cross before me;
No turning back, no turning back.

Though none go with me, still I will follow;
Though none go with me, still I will follow;
Though none go with me, still I will follow;
No turning back, no turning back